Children's Min...y

Children's Ministry has a commitment to provide the resources and training needed to help busy children's workers develop their ability to evangelise and disciple the children in their community.

Children's Ministry Guides are short, easy-to-read books offering practical insights into key areas of children's ministry. They complement the other resources and training opportunities available from Children's Ministry including:

- conferences
- training days
- distance learning course
- undated, activity-based, Bible-centred teaching programme
- books of ready-to-use ideas
- books of opinion and wisdom from children's ministry practitioners
- CDs and music books of children's praise songs
- supporting resources.

For more details about the Children's Ministry range of resources visit www.childrensministry.co.uk or call 01323 437748.

Other titles in the series:

Storytelling

RUTH ALLISTON

with
Andy Back, Jenny Brown,
Cathy Kyte, Sue Price

Series edited by Sue Price

EASTBOURNE

ISBN 1 84291 034 5

Published by
KINGSWAY COMMUNICATIONS LTD
Lottbridge Drove, Eastbourne, BN23 6NT, England.
Email: books@kingsway.co.uk

Book design and production for the publishers by
Bookprint Creative Services, P.O. Box 827, BN21 3YJ, England.
Printed in Great Britain.

For Noah, Daisy and Danny,
who make storytelling such joy,
and for the grandchildren soon to be born
who will be able to share it with us.

Contents

Acknowledgements

I acknowledge that I could never have written this without the wisdom and guidance of the Children's Ministry team who have taught me so much, and with whom work is such pleasure. Their encouragement is a constant spur to try harder and do better, and to be part of this team is one of the joys of my life.

For many years I have practised storytelling in all its various forms and facets on my family. It is a sheer delight to see their enjoyment of storytelling and creative participation now forming part of their own families, as it should. Their encouragement to write what we have shared is appreciated more than they will ever know.

Ruth Alliston

Introduction

Books and recounted stories may seem old-fashioned to some, but they provide opportunities for children to develop their own pictures and images. It has been scientifically proved that this mental development helps to exercise and grow the brain. Most children today take in other people's ideas and images from many sources, and seem unable to form their own. Those of us who were brought up with the joy of being told stories know the foundations of imagination and play that these form, leading to creative ideas and the ability to work things out for ourselves.

In our rushed lives, there seems little time for storytelling. The lone watching of television programmes and videos is no substitute. Many of the modern activities available to children today are solo activities, and children lose out from having close, loving contact and human interaction.

Visually and aurally children can become over-stimulated

and jaded by an early age, as the intensive and constant stream of images and sounds blaze into their minds from outside. Many are not taught or allowed to occupy themselves, or just sit and work things out quietly. Parents are under increasing pressure to provide exciting and stimulating after-school activities so that their children will not miss out or fall behind. One of the results is that physically and mentally, children are often tired, and gentler and less aggressive pursuits, like simple storytelling, are an ideal remedy.

Simple storytelling, with minimum pictures and action, relying mainly on the voice and expression of the storyteller and the imagination of the child, has a very important place, particularly in one-to-one or small group reading or telling – i.e. at the end of a busy day, after a boisterous game, to create an oasis of calm or escape from reality for a few minutes. Even if children are not used to having stories told or read in this way, they can be trained to enjoy them by listening to short, expressive stories that create mind pictures.

However, for larger groups, where you may have a teaching purpose or particular focus that you want children to remember, you will need to employ additional learning style features to reach every child, and enable them to grasp your point. Even stories told just for fun to larger groups of children will probably need extra features, to ensure that everyone is able to enjoy them. You will find plenty of suggestions for these in the following age group chapters.

At its best, storytelling is a deeply satisfying and enjoyable shared experience: a voyage of discovery, during which the thrills and joys of deep communication are given and received. At its worst, storytelling is an unmitigated disaster of rushed preparation, interruptions, distractions, apathy, boredom, disorder and riot, descending into utter chaos. Whatever your experience to date on this scale of extremes, it is hoped that you will find this book helpful, because one thing is certain: if you are working with children, sooner or later you will need to tell a story.

You may have picked up this book in desperation, having been asked to tell a story for the very first time. You may feel that you have no skills or abilities, and fear you will not be able to communicate well or hold children's attention. Where do I begin? How can I achieve a good result quickly? How can I stem this rising tide of panic? The last chapter in this book may help you through the initial storytelling experience. Perhaps as you fast-forward through easy-fix ways to tell a story, you may find yourself enjoying the adventure so much that you will go back and look deeper into the craft of storytelling. You will find there is some repetition in the three chapters on storytelling for different age groups. Where the same point is valid across more than one age group, I have included it in each chapter for the sake of completeness.

You may simply have run out of ideas, and cannot think of any more ways to tell stories, or even know what stories to tell. God expects and encourages us to give our very best. Children, too, expect the best. Today, as never before, our children are bombarded with a huge variety of media for learning, taking in information, relaxation and play. Some are of excellent quality, others dismal, and many in between. It's important to be familiar with what our children are exposed to on a daily basis through TV programmes, radio, CDs, videos, toys, games, interactive games, CD Roms and Internet activity.

Children's workers are among the busiest of people in churches, and there is precious little time for refreshing, reading, thinking, looking at new ideas and re-thinking old ones. If the idea of yet more things to do makes your heart sink, resist adding discouragement to the list. You know full well that you cannot continue to run the engine on empty. The fact that you are reading this introduction shows your willingness to give more, even though you feel depleted. Ask God to use this book to refresh and regenerate your desire to reach children for God, and help them find their place in his plan. You can help them know that they are part of his story, deeply embedded in his heart and here in his world for a purpose.

Ruth Alliston

1. Why Tell Stories?

There are many good reasons to tell stories, and we need not think of storytelling as just a children's activity. Traditionally, that has never been the case.

- Stories affirm group identities. They fulfil a need to know our place and feel a part of a family, united against loneliness and the harsh realities of life.
- Stories help to answer the deep questions of the soul: Who am I? Where is God? Why am I here? How do I fit into the world? When will good triumph? What will happen when I die?
- Stories stir emotions, and help give voice to feelings.
- Stories help make sense of the known world, and open us up to new ideas from the outside world.
- Stories can act as a definer of group boundaries and rules within a community, and aid in socialising its members.

- Stories have an important place, alongside food, water, air, love, hope and faith. Indeed, adults may be in greater need of stories because of their pain, pride, anxieties and fears.
- Stories have powerful healing qualities, as they cross barriers of prejudice and hate.
- Stories influence the way we think.
- Stories help listeners get to know the teller as they reveal themselves in the telling.
- Stories enable listeners to feel cared for by the teller, as part of the group or family.
- Stories fascinate us, and whatever catches our interest can be an effective learning tool.
- Stories permit potentially troublesome or taboo subjects to be explored, as the views expressed are not necessarily those of the teller.
- Stories stimulate thoughts, imagination and creativity, leading to play, conversation, solutions and action.
- Stories, when powerfully told, stay with the listener for a long time.
- Stories encourage listeners to become involved and, having owned the story, to be satisfied.
- Stories allow listeners to acknowledge and express their emotions safely within the group.
- Stories are a vehicle for passing on information.
- Stories help us identify with other people's situations, and promote caring and understanding.
- Stories can be used to prepare people for difficult or life-changing events, such as migration, war, illness,

death, and effectively improve mental, physical and emotional abilities to cope.

- Stories give pleasure.
- Stories enable the teller to experience and enjoy the powerful dynamics at work when telling a story, and know the pleasure of performing well, being heard and approved.

In addition:

- Bible stories show a cameo of God at work in people's lives, and what happens as a result.
- Bible stories allow us to examine our own lives, and line them up with the lives of those in the story.
- Bible stories point to God.
- Bible stories turn us to God.
- Bible stories help us make sense of life and eternity in ways that other stories cannot.
- Bible stories reach into our spirits and encourage change and growth.
- Bible stories convey biblical truth.
- Bible stories foster faith in a big God who is in control of the universe.
- Bible stories offer hope of salvation.
- Bible stories lead us to praise and worship God.
- Bible stories encourage prayer.
- Bible stories are powerful because they are God's stories.
- Bible stories invite a response from us.

Convinced you should tell stories? I hope you are!

2. Storytelling Past and Present

Storytelling has a long history from the dawn of time. Storytellers were important and valued tribe members, holding the history of the tribe and a guarantee of its future. Storytellers were often members of the same family, and the stories were faithfully learned, under long apprenticeship, to be passed down from generation to generation.

Although the village storyteller, who held the complete and corporate story of the village and its people, may have vanished in most places in the world, the telling and the keeping of the tale is perhaps just as important to us as ever. Where stories and storytelling have been lost to a people or culture, a great deal more is also lost, to their detriment and ours. For some peoples, colonisation and urbanisation have wrecked their traditions, culture, native tongue, dialect, customs, traditions and folklore. It was once deemed that primitive peoples have no civilisation, and nothing of worth to tell. Nothing could be further from the truth.

Many countries have a history of travelling storytellers, paid in money or kind, to tell their tales. More recently, this is being revived in different parts of the world. Stories are being recalled, rescued, discovered and delighted in once more. There is an old saying: 'When an old person dies, it is as though a whole library has gone up in smoke.' So much has been lost, but there is still so much worth telling. Today, family storytelling in homes may not be as great as it once was, but radio and TV still feature stories in children's programmes and drama. Also, storytelling in communities can be found in schools, theatres, cinemas, hospitals, libraries, churches and community centres. The tradition of telling tales is also adapting itself to an electronic age. Although some things are lost in this form of telling, a cursory surf of the Internet will reveal that both the teller and the tales survive and thrive in today's global village.

There are countless vehicles traditionally used around the world to tell stories, some sadly lost. We only have room to look at a few of them here.

Sagas

The most well known sagas are the heroic prose narratives written in Old Norse, the best of which were written down in Iceland in the twelfth and thirteenth centuries. The stirring tales of adventurers, wars, migrations and other deeds were drawn from ancient Scandinavian oral traditions, including fictionalised accounts of the acts of Norwegian kings, such as Snorri Sturluson's *Heimskringla*, heroic legends of the pagan past, *Volsungasaga*, and whole family sagas.

Epics

Epics are long, narrative poems based on history and legend, extolling the virtues of heroes. They cover the range of human experience, including love, war, compassion, self-sacrifice, courage, betrayal, patience, respect for the elderly and reverence for the sacred. The *Iliad* and the *Odyssey* of Homer, written in the eighth century BC in Greece, are the earliest epics of Western literature. English literature examples include the Old English *Beowolf*, written in the eighth century AD, Spenser's *Faerie Queene* (1589–1596), and Milton's *Paradise Lost* (1667). Epics were performed by trained storytellers at festivals, wakes, funerals and other public events. Epics were the great films of their time, painted in people's minds and told against a backdrop of flames, warmth and community.

Chronicles

The Jewish chronicles

The Hebrew name for these books is *Dibrî Hayyammîm*, which means 'events of the times'. The Greek *Paraleipomena* has the meaning of 'things left over', from the Book of

Kings. These chronicles comprise two Old Testament books, covering the history of Judah from the creation to the end of the Babylonian exile in 538 BC. It is thought they were possibly written by Ezra in the fourth century BC, and originally formed a continuous history with the books of Ezra and Nehemiah. After opening with genealogies from Adam, they describe the reigns of David and Solomon and the succeeding kings of Judah, with special emphasis on the building of the Temple in Jerusalem.

The British chronicles

These comprise two books. The first chronicle was compiled by Nennius in the ninth century AD, sourced from surviving oral traditions and Irish and Roman written records. It covers the arrival of the earliest settlers into Britain after the Flood. This first chronicle considers the origins of other European nations, and traces them back to Noah through his son, Japheth. The second of the British chronicles was a twelfth-century translation by Geoffrey of Monmouth into Latin of an earlier work written in the ancient British language. Until the arrival of the early Britons, the British Isles had most likely been uninhabited, and this second chronicle covers the history of those early Britons. It deals with the Roman conquest of Britain, and finishes with the last of the ancient British kings, who died in the seventh century AD.

The Irish chronicles

These trace the arrival of peoples in Ireland over a long

period of time, from 1484 BC. Some came as invaders, others as refugees, all bringing their own tales and histories. It has been increasingly possible, through archaeology and other works of history, to check out points of reference to verify their accuracy.

Anglo-Saxon chronicles

These are a collection of seven manuscripts, reputedly begun by King Alfred of Wessex in AD 890, and continued by monks living in England between the ninth and twelfth centuries. They are written in Anglo-Saxon, and cover a period of one thousand years, from 60 BC to AD 1154.

Genealogies

Genealogies were very important to ancient peoples. They were kept accurately, and known by heart to those whose job it was to preserve them. To tamper with them was an extremely serious offence. It has been found that tribes that have no written language have extraordinary memories, as they rely on oral tradition passed on from generation to generation. Two things that are passed down very accurately in those tribes are: genealogies (family trees) and sagas.

The Book of Genesis records ten family histories, each beginning: 'These are the generations of . . .' These are the genealogies accurately told to and remembered by Hebrew slaves, when they had no written language. Genesis also contains sagas of people like Noah, Abraham and Isaac, faithfully passed on from memory, by oral tradition.

The Saxon genealogies

The Saxons began their prolonged migration to England with Angles and Jutes around the middle of the fifth century AD, having been invited by Vortigern, King of the Britons. The Saxons were a Germanic people living around the Baltic coast. They also migrated to northern Germany and France. Although distinct in every way from Britons, there are genealogical records to show that Saxons shared a common heritage with Britons, Irish and other European communities, going back to the time of the Flood and Babel, when peoples were scattered.

Stones and memorials

The Code of Hammurabi, King of Babylon (1792–1750 BC), is inscribed on stone excavated from Susa, the winter capital of Persia (now Iran). This is a collection of Babylonian laws written in the Akkadian language, and tells a story of those times that would otherwise be beyond our reach. Also discovered at Susa are inscriptions of Artaxerxes II (404–358 BC).

Walk around any old church or its graveyard and read the inscriptions. Each one has its own tantalising story: partial, yet complete in itself.

Songs

In every people group and culture, songs are sung. These

24

contain history, stories both true and fictional. Every known experience has been sung about through pop, ballads, music hall, opera, negro spirituals, West End or Broadway musical hits, and many other kinds of song. Some great hymns and Christian songs tell Scripture in story form, e.g. Charles Wesley's *And can it be?* and John Newton's *Glorious things of thee are spoken*. There are specialised songs, with rhythm for prisoners to march to and break rocks, dreaming of freedom, and sea shanties, with rhythm for sailors to work the ropes and cables, dreaming of home. In olden times, there were groups of travelling troubadors, who took their sung tales around the world, enriching the lives of others and bringing back yet more tales to tell.

In some African cultures, there are groups of singers who tell stories, with a master singer to lead them. He sings a line, and others in the group respond with comment, interjection, observation and humour. Dance is a by-product, with hands and feet to help the rhythm, and instruments are sometimes used also.

Antiphonal singing is a common style of folk song in some parts of China. Lyrics are sung in turn by two or more singers, and tell wondrous tales. These include love songs used during courtship. Every stage of the courtship is included in the lengthy song, with humorous exchanges. Each song tells an individual story, as every couple is different. In some places in China, guests in someone's home may be greeted or sent away with songs. Guests are expected to reply in like manner. People may stop to chat to each other or tell a tale, and choose song as the medium for their conversation. In some areas, court cases were carried out in song form.

Miracle plays

Miracle plays were medieval European dramas based on religious themes. In England, they flourished in the fourteenth and early fifteenth centuries, and were based mainly on Scripture. In France, miracle plays were usually based on the lives of the saints, and Bible stories were told in the form of mystery plays. Few ordinary people at this time were literate, and plays provided a visual enactment of stories they could not read for themselves. Miracle plays were originally performed in churches on religious holidays, especially Corpus Christi and Whitsuntide. As they became increasingly secularised in both form and content, they were eventually performed in public market-places by trade guilds, using mobile stages. Some almost com-plete cycles of miracle plays have survived, the best known being those from York, Chester, Coventry and Wakefield.

Morality plays

Morality plays were a form of popular religious drama, fashionable in England and France from the late fourteenth to the late sixteenth centuries. Morality plays were similar in content and purpose to medieval sermons, and were dramatised allegories of good and evil fighting for man's soul. Examples include *The Pride of Life*, *The Castle of Perseverance*, and *Everyman*. At the time of the Reformation in England, they provided a vehicle for dramatising the religious issues at stake.

Chronicle plays

Chronicle plays were the successors to the medieval morality plays that were popular in England during the Elizabethan era. Some examples are Marlowe's *Edward II*, produced in 1592, and Shakespeare's *King John*, produced around 1596. Many of the plots used in chronicle plays were taken from Holinshed's *Chronicles* (1578).

Other plays and dramas

Most communities have used plays and drama in various forms to tell tales of their history, legends, fables, folklore, gods and adventures. These have sometimes been performed by actors from within the community, or by travelling bands of actors staging theatrical events. Puppets, peep shows, magic, dressing up in animal or bird costumes, and forceful symbols, such as Chinese dragons, are other examples of stories with great meaning for their watchers and listeners.

Oral rhymes

Few of the rhymes we know as nursery rhymes were

originally intended for children. They are a collection of unrelated fragments of satire, lampoons, proverbs, popular ballads and songs of their day, political and other jokes composed over centuries. In their original form, they were mostly oral, and only later came to be written down. Each tells a story of their time, passed around by travellers, and eagerly accepted by the communities they passed through.

Poetry

Poetry is a powerful storyteller. Like music, it bypasses obstacles and goes straight to the emotions. With its rhythm and breadth of words, it captures thoughts and feelings that people struggle to express. Poetry has numerous forms worldwide, and is present in most communities, whether oral or written. Apart from published or oral poems known to exist, many people who would not necessarily class themselves as poets tell stories, both personal and communal, through their secret poetry.

Music and dance

Music has many forms, and quickly reaches every part of complex human beings, bringing the capacity for enlightenment, change and healing. Music is one of the vehicles for storytelling, e.g. Benjamin Britten's *Sea Interludes*, Handel's *Arrival of the Queen of Sheba*, Prokofiev's *Peter and the Wolf*.

Dance is a very effective storyteller, especially when

combined with music. Stories told through ballet, such as *Swan Lake* and *Giselle* are well-known. However, dance is manifested in as many ways as there are communities, from Hawaii to Helsinki and Morocco to Mexico.

Art

From their earliest days on earth, without written language, our ancestors sought to describe their lives and surroundings in picture form. These stories were most often told in cave art, representing those people's known world of animals, flora and fauna, and their struggles and battles. One of the most impressive examples of cave art in Europe is in the Chauvet-Pont-d'Arc cave in the Ardèche, France. It contains hundreds of paintings and engravings that tell us vivid stories from that time.

Later, as artists were able to invest time and energy in exploring other materials, stories through art were displayed in other ways. Many Roman mosaics, still with their glorious colours and pictures intact, have been uncovered for us to read and wonder at. These non-verbal stories give a vibrant and different perspective, and add to our knowledge of people's lives, their fears, hopes and dreams.

A trip through any art gallery in the world will reveal stories from the past in fascinating and vivid ways that make the people of those times instantly recognisable and real to us.

Stories are also expressed through the medium of

pottery, tapestry and sculpture. Fabric wall coverings, orig-inally used only to cover and warm damp walls and floors, and keep draughts at bay, gradually evolved into more decorative and colourful tapestries. Their pictures and symbols told stories from people's lives. The Bayeux tapes-try in northern France is an embroidered linen strip 69 metres long, worked by many women. Created in the eleventh century, it tells the story of King Harold's visit to Normandy, and ends with the Battle of Hastings in 1066.

Other more humble designs were sewn as samplers. Samplers date back some four hundred years, or even earlier. They were traditionally sewn by young girls, learning dif-ferent stitches, to prepare them for a lifetime of sewing for husbands and families. As time went on, these became more elaborate, with names, motifs, proverbs and family histories. Each one told a unique story, not least because of the blood, sweat and tears shed by the children who strug-gled to create them, probably no older than twelve.

All across the world, from South American tribal hats and shawls to Iraqi carpet makers you will find stories and symbols in woven fabric. Today, these are often bought as tourist gifts, with little thought for the stories they repre-sent.

Christianity has an artistic history stretching back to its earliest days, when Christians took refuge from persecu-tion in the catacombs of Rome, and expressed their faith in pictures and symbols. Christians have always used art to communicate characteristics of faith, truth, hope and love, and portray Bible stories in picture form. For example

Kitchen Scene with Christ in the House with Mary and Martha by Diego Velázquez, and *Christ Walking on the Water* by Alessandro Magnasco. In *The Resurrected Christ*, Piero della Francesca painted the risen Christ standing in the centre, effectively dividing the picture in half. He has Jesus standing with one foot still in the grave, and all the trees in that half of the picture are barren. The trees in the other half of the picture are in full leaf. A story shouting blazing truth, without a single spoken word.

Christian art is also expressed through the icons of the Orthodox Church, in tapestry, sculpture, stained glass, and on walls and floors. The Sistine Chapel, principal chapel of the Vatican in Rome, is famous for its Renaissance interior decoration, with murals by Botticelli, Ghirlandaio and Perugino, and the ceiling and roof by Michelangelo. These non-verbal stories have a teaching role, as well as helping to encourage and lift believers to God in worship.

The richly ornamented pages of books, like the Lindisfarne Gospels, copied into Latin around AD 700, combine to make a stunning telling of the stories of Jesus, and represent a lifetime's dedication to the glory of God by monks and others that we can only marvel at.

Other religions have their own storytelling traditions in art and artefacts, picture stories, puppets and dances, particularly in celebrating their religious festivals. In some Indian homes, adults would study their sacred texts and, instead of reading them with or to children, the child watched the adult's face and hands during the storytelling, and the adult watched the child. The dreamtime stories

31

and oral traditions of Aboriginal Australians are well documented. With and without verbal communication, people have devised creative and effective ways to tell what needs to be told.

Stained glass

In northern Europe, stained glass windows in churches were used from the twelfth century onwards. Many of the best examples are in France, and tell Bible stories and episodes from the lives of saints. There are also many examples of the delights of heaven and the agonies of hell. These were picture stories for people who had no access to literature, or the ability to read it.

Home fireside or bedtime storytelling

This unique form of storytelling has a long and honourable history. Twenty-first-century life in so called Westernised cultures has damaged and eroded home storytelling, but its value is being increasingly recognised and huge efforts made to reclaim it. Storytelling is still very much alive in many homes throughout the world. The stories told have similarities from human experience, religion, history and folklore. Who can reckon their effect and future worth on children? This, perhaps the simplest form of storytelling, unifies families, provides a safe haven, a place to ask questions and work out answers, and can inspire creative processes for good.

3. Jesus the Storyteller

There is an abundance of excellent storytellers, past and present, from whom we can learn more about the craft of storytelling, but the master storyteller must be Jesus. The most hurried read through the Gospels shows that whenever Jesus told a story, people listened avidly. Wherever he went, they flocked to hear him. How did he come to be such a brilliant storyteller? Apart from any natural God-given talent, he probably improved his craft from early years onwards. Jesus keenly observed people, and knew them from the inside out. He had an easy identity within the close-knit Jewish community, and was able to draw on the intensely rich and fertile vein of his culture.

When Jesus returned from Egypt with his parents, they settled in the small, quiet town of Nazareth in Galilee, well away from the new King Herod's eyes. Although little is known of his early history, we know that Jesus grew up in this ordinary place as part of an ordinary family. Theirs was a simple home, and although not poverty stricken, life was not always easy. Joseph was a carpenter, who most likely had a workshop at home. As a small boy, Jesus probably 'helped' his father with small tasks and played as he watched Joseph work. Jesus became the eldest son, and brother to other children in the family. Mary would have worked hard within the home, looking after her children, feeding and clothing them, fetching water with other women and being part of her community. Children were taught to respect their mothers and not bring shame on them. We can see from Jesus' adult attitude to women that he learned that lesson well.

Faith and family life were intertwined as parents brought up their children. Jesus would have been encouraged to ask questions and to explore the Jewish faith and history. For example, when visiting places where God had done something special for his people, Jesus would have seen that they were marked with large stones.

In days to come when your son asks you, 'What does this mean?' say to him, 'With a mighty hand the Lord brought us out of Egypt, out of the land of slavery.' (Exodus 13:14)

So Joshua called together the twelve men he had appointed from the Israelites, one from each tribe, and said to them, 'Go over before the ark of the Lord your God into the middle of the Jordan. Each of you is to take up a stone on his shoulder, according to the number of the tribes of the Israelites, to serve as a sign among you. In the future, when your children ask you, 'What do these stones mean?' tell them that the flow of the Jordan was cut off before the ark of the covenant of the Lord. When it crossed the Jordan, the waters of the Jordan were cut off. These stones are to be a memorial to the people of Israel for ever.' (Joshua 4:4–7)

It's not hard to believe that such stirring stories would excite a young child, provoking more questions and more stories.

The great religious festivals of the Jewish faith were marked with special ceremonies and celebrations. At every festival, Jesus would have heard the amazing stories of God's hand on his people, leading and guiding. A brief look at this rich source of material will help us see how Jesus learned his craft of storytelling.

At **Passover**, the father would always ask the eldest child, 'Why do we have this service?' Jesus, as the eldest child, would have taken responsibility each year as storyteller for the whole family, recounting the rousing and terrifying tale of the exodus from slavery, as he had been taught. There is no biblical record of Jesus telling stories to children, but undoubtedly he did at home, with his younger brothers and sisters.

Passover was celebrated in the home, but by the time of Jesus it was the main pilgrim festival and celebrated in Jerusalem. It was probably not possible for everyone to travel to Jerusalem each year, but certainly Jesus went when he was twelve years old. Although we are only given a snapshot of that time, it must have been a memorable occasion for him, not least because he was aware of his identity. Apart from being Joseph's and Mary's obedient son, he was also the obedient Son of God.

Israel's main religious festivals were connected with the farming calendar and seasons. The celebration of **Firstfruits** was held on the last day of the Festival of Unleavened Bread during Passover. The first sheaf of barley was presented to God as his right. Jesus and his family, although not farmers, would have been part of this celebration and honouring of God.

Weeks, or Pentecost, as it later became known, came at the end of the grain harvest, 50 days after Passover and Firstfruits. The priest offered two loaves of bread made from new flour, with animal sacrifices. It was a great time of celebration, with plentiful food, thanksgiving, colour and rejoicing. Jesus, as a normal boy, would have enjoyed it greatly, as well as absorbing the richness of his heritage.

Festivals and the day of the new moon every month were announced by a blast of ram's horn trumpets, and celebrated to remind God's people of his orderly creation. Treated as a Sabbath, with no work, special meals were prepared and eaten, and the people taught from God's word. On the first day of the seventh month, people celebrated **Trumpets**, or New Year as it became known, and the trumpets sounded very loudly! Young boys would have delighted in the noise, processions and special celebrations as people worshipped God together.

The **Day of Atonement** or *Yom Kippur* was the day when the whole nation confessed their sins, asking God's forgiveness and cleansing. It's not difficult to imagine the young Jesus taking everything in and watching wide-eyed as the ceremonies progressed.

The high priest, in his fine white linen robes, first offered sacrifice for his own sin and those of the priests. Then he offered another sacrifice for the sins of the people. Only on this day could the high priest enter the 'holy of holies', the inner and most sacred part of the Temple. So great was their fear of God that in case the high priest was overcome and rendered senseless, or killed by the presence of God, he had a rope tied around his ankle, so that he could be pulled out if necessary. There, in the presence of God, he sprinkled blood from the sacrifice. Taking a goat, known as the scapegoat, he laid hands on it and set it free, as a sign that the people's sins were taken away.

Tabernacles was the most popular and joyous of all the celebrations, held during autumn after the fruit harvest. Children especially enjoyed Tabernacles, as families camped out on their roof tops, in gardens, or in tents and huts. Tabernacles reminded God's people of the time when Israel had camped in the desert. The festival included the pouring out of water and prayers, asking God's favour for rain for the coming season.

The festival of **Dedication** or **Lights** remembered the cleansing and rededication of the second Temple. In 165 BC Judas Maccabaeus purified the Temple and gave it back to God, after its desecration by a Syrian ruler, Antiochus IV. Each evening during the festival, lamps were placed and lit in homes and in the synagogue. What stories would have been told about Judas Maccabaeus!

Purim celebrated the time when Esther and her cousin, Mordecai, saved God's people from massacre during the reign of Xerxes. Purim means 'lots' and refers to the nasty villain of the piece, Haman, who as the king's chief minister, drew lots to decide which day the Jews should be killed. It gave children plenty of opportunity for drama, with grisly bits, in one of the most colourful stories in the Bible. It's not hard to see Jesus relishing his part in it.

The regular **Sabbath**, rest day, was intended by God to be a day when his people remembered and worshipped him. The Sabbath service in the synagogue consisted of reading from the Scriptures in scroll form. They were kept in a chest or ark, and handled by the synagogue leaders. The Scriptures were written and read in Hebrew. By Jesus' time, most Jews spoke Aramaic, and a translation was given. Prayers were offered, and sometimes there was a sermon. Jesus would have gone regularly to the synagogue and sat with his mother and siblings, hearing God's word read aloud.

These festivals and celebrations were an integral part of Jesus' upbringing, and influenced not only his commitment to his heavenly Father, but also gave vivid colour and action to the stories he had been taught from infancy.

Jesus would have been taught at home, before going to school at the local synagogue when he was about six years old, to be further trained in Scripture and godly ways. Jesus would have had friends of his own age with whom he played and learned. As an adult, it's probable that Jesus spoke from personal experience when he described children play-acting stories of weddings and funerals in the market-place.

'To what can I compare this generation? They are like children sitting in the market-places and calling out to others: "We played the flute for you, and you did not dance; we sang a dirge, and you did not mourn."' (Matthew 11:16–17)

Although Jesus' family was not directly involved in farming, the whole of the community depended on the land, rainfall and seasonal changes. Jesus grew up being very much aware of what and how things grew.

The Sea of Galilee was a rich source of fish for people nearby. Jesus must have watched men fishing many times, and reflected on their way of life. His observations and experiences shaped not only his knowledge of people, but his storytelling repertoire too.

When choosing topics for stories, Jesus revealed his knowledge of crop farming, fishing, vine tending and animal husbandry. Through his stories, he also showed his understanding of people's feelings as they coped with good times and bad. It is believed that Joseph died when Jesus was comparatively young. As the eldest son, he would have taken responsibility for his mother and the rest of the family. Jesus knew how pressure, worry and grief weighed people down. Jesus could speak about those things with understanding and sympathy.

The Sabbath had become so hidebound with man-made

traditions that were impossible to keep. Jesus saw the impossible demands put on his friends and neighbours by hypocritical teachers of the law in every aspect of their lives, including food laws, tithing and ritual cleansing. Jesus' later condemnation of scribes and Pharisees over the Sabbath through stories and direct confrontation came from his lifelong observation of seeing people trying to please God in ways that were totally unnecessary. His stories, while often pleasing ordinary people, deeply offended those who tried to make themselves important in the eyes of others.

With comparatively few words, Jesus could create pictures in the minds of his listeners. He could think quickly on his feet, and reply to questions with both humour and incisive soundbites.

What can we learn from his model of storytelling?

Jesus used parables to make his point

Jesus often used parables when telling stories, and it seems that people didn't always understand them. Parables place another meaning alongside the obvious story. Sometimes the point was very clear to those who needed to see it. At other times, it seems that Jesus deliberately obscured his point, or didn't explain it. This may have been because he didn't want to risk being arrested before his work was finished, or perhaps because he knew people were not ready to hear the whole truth. Privately, Jesus taught his disciples the meaning of his parables. Mainly, people heard Jesus' stories at their own level of understanding or enjoyment, but could also go away and think more about what they had heard.

> Again he said, 'What shall we say the kingdom of God is like, or what parable shall we use to describe it? It is like a mustard seed, which is the smallest seed you plant in the ground. Yet when planted, it grows and becomes the largest of all garden plants, with such big branches that the birds of the air can perch in its shade.'
>
> With many similar parables Jesus spoke the word to them, as much as they could understand. He did not say anything to them without using a parable. But when he was alone with his own disciples, he explained everything. (Mark 4:30–34)

Jesus' point was that the kingdom of God introduced by him seemed so tiny and insignificant that he was rejected and despised by those who looked for greater things. He and his disciples appeared to be poor specimens. But, just as a tiny, insignificant mustard seed grows to massive proportions, God's kingdom will grow and be seen in its true greatness and power.

Many children's stories are told in parable form, e.g. Red Riding Hood and the Big Bad Wolf. The point that it's not a good idea to go off with a big, bad wolf, however nice they seem, doesn't have to be spelled out to children for them to enjoy the story, or for some of them to get the point. However, the story can be explained in terms of stranger-danger if the storyteller thinks it appropriate.

Jesus used plain, clear imagery and familiar things to make his point

Jesus drew on ordinary, everyday objects and situations to make his point clear. In Luke 15, the Pharisees complain that Jesus mixed with the worst of sinners. Pharisees would not go near such people, for fear of contamination. They believed that if Jesus was a teacher and rabbi, then he shouldn't either. To see him relaxed and having fun with such people mystified and angered them.

Jesus told three stories, using familiar objects and situations to make the same point: the contrast between God's extravagant love and the exclusivity of the Pharisees.

1. A good shepherd takes responsibility for straying sheep. He leaves those who are already safe, and searches until he finds the lost sheep. Not only does he bring it home joyfully, but throws a party with his friends to celebrate the wanderer's return. Razor sharp, Jesus made his point:

   > I tell you that in the same way there will be more rejoicing in heaven over one sinner who repents than over ninety-nine righteous persons who do not need to repent. (Luke 15:7)

2. A woman loses a coin. Jesus' listeners knew that every coin is precious. This situation would be familiar to

them. Many of their homes had no windows and earthen floors, making small coins difficult to find. When the woman found the coin, she also threw a party. Jesus made his point:

> In the same way, I tell you, there is rejoicing in the presence of the angels of God over one sinner who repents. (Luke 15:10)

3. The sharing out of a father's estate. Everyone understood the inheritance laws laid down in Deuteronomy 21:17, and that these often caused friction in families (Luke 12:13). The law stated that in certain circumstances, while the father was still alive, he could give his eldest son a double portion of his inheritance but would retain the income from it until his death. For a younger son to request his portion before his father's death would be deeply disapproved of. When Jesus finished this third story, he had no need to spell out his point. He was clearly understood by all.

When we tell stories, we can use those things with which children are familiar and from our culture to make our point and help children understand truth:

- belonging to a family
- home life
- friends/relationships
- pets and other animals

- everyday events
- everyday actions
- feelings – love, hate, fear, jealousy, anger, sadness, kindness, betrayal
- surroundings – where I live
- school life
- funny things that happen to us
- special times and celebrations.

Jesus usually made just one point

Jesus didn't complicate his stories with three or more points. One at a time was enough for people to think about, as in the story of the wise and foolish builders.

> Therefore, everyone who hears these words of mine and puts them into practice is like a wise man who built his house on the rock. The rain came down, the streams rose, and the winds blew and beat against that house; yet it did not fall, because it had its foundation on the rock. But everyone who hears these words of mine and does not put them to practice is like a foolish man who built his house on sand. The rain came down, the streams rose, and the winds blew and beat against that house, and it fell with a great crash. (Matthew 7:24–27)

Jesus' one point is that the man who hears these words of Jesus and lives accordingly is building upon a rock; the man who does not is building on sand, with consequences that were well-known to his listeners.

44

We can follow Jesus' example and make a simple point from the stories we tell, for example: 'Jesus wants us to do what he says.'

Jesus knew the needs of his listeners, and matched his stories to them

Religious leaders criticised people's efforts to keep the Law, and used it like a cricket bat around the head, to no good effect. People felt that Jesus was on their side in their struggles with religious authorities and life under Roman rule. Of course, they didn't understand fully who he was or what he was doing, but instinctively they were drawn to his kind and fair way of dealing with people. They also enjoyed the discomfort of the teachers of the Law and the Pharisees, when they tried to trip Jesus up with questions. Jesus understood all that, and more.

Jesus told the story of the Pharisee and the tax collector in the Temple (Luke 18:9–14) directly to those 'who were confident of their own righteousness and looked down on everybody else'. People could well imagine such a scene in the Temple, even if they had not actually seen it happen. It probably caused some merriment and embarrassment for different listeners. Jesus knew that people needed to hear that those who call on God from the heart for mercy will receive mercy and forgiveness, and that those who merely parade their good works will not be heard.

45

Jesus didn't explain every last detail of his stories

In the story Jesus told about the man who was travelling from Jerusalem to Jericho when he was ambushed by thieves (Luke 10:30–37), Jesus didn't say why the man was travelling alone, or what his business was in Jericho. Nor did he specify the man's injuries, or what the Samaritan was doing on that road.

Too many details can detract from the point we are trying to make, and take up valuable time. We also risk losing children's interest before the story is finished, or getting bogged down in trivia. Children listening to a well-told story can fill in spaces for themselves if they feel it necessary.

Jesus used the minimum number of words to give maximum impact

After listening to his disciples arguing, Jesus shocked them and turned their understanding of greatness on its head:

> You know that those who are regarded as rulers of the Gentiles lord it over them, and their high officials exercise authority over them. Not so with you. Instead, whoever wants to become great among you must be your servant, and whoever wants to be first must be slave of all. For even the Son of Man did not come to be served, but to serve, and to give his life as a ransom for many. (Mark 10:42–45)

46

Children are used to hearing a torrent of language all day long, at school, at home, after-school activities, from the TV. Their faces show many times that words wash over them without penetrating. Even adults 'listening' to sermons are often elsewhere inside their heads. Think carefully about how much to say. Make the best use of language, and keep it as brief as possible.

Jesus involved his listeners in the story

The expert in the Law who questioned Jesus (Luke 10:25–37) became so involved in the story about the man who had been beaten up, that he found himself approving of the good helper's actions, without realising that he was supposed to be an enemy. Jesus, never one to miss an opportunity, asked the innocent yet deadly question, 'Which of these three do you think was a neighbour to the man who fell into the hands of robbers?' One can imagine the 'expert' grinding out his own punch-line to the delight of the crowd, 'The one who had mercy on him.'

Jesus didn't do this to make the man look stupid, but to get his point through in the most efficient way to someone who was blind to the truth.

Like Jesus, we can make our stories interesting and exciting so that children become involved and connected with the characters. This will help lead them to acknowledge truth.

Jesus invites his listeners to respond to his teaching point

Taking the example of the good Samaritan story, having heard the expert in the Law acknowledge his teaching point, Jesus told him to go and do likewise.

After using ordinary items from home to make a point about himself, the Light of the World yet to be revealed, Jesus invited a response from his listeners.

> Do you bring in a lamp to put it under a bowl or a bed? Instead, don't you put it on its stand? For whatever is hidden is meant to be disclosed, and whatever is concealed is meant to be brought out in the open. If anyone has ears to hear, let him hear. (Mark 4:21–22)

When teachers of the Law and Pharisees brought a woman caught in adultery to Jesus, their aim was not just to make an exhibition of her but to trick Jesus into a wrong answer. When Jesus made his graphic point and the men had slunk away, without harshness or condemnation, he invited the woman to go and leave her sin (John 8:11).

Jesus didn't always invite a response from his listeners, and we don't need to, either. But there are times when it will be important for children to respond and take a step forward in obedience and understanding.

4. Storytelling with Three- to Five-year-olds

Why should I tell stories?

Chapter one gives some good reasons for telling stories to children, but one of the most important reasons is because stories are a very effective vehicle for enjoyment and communication of values and ideas in an easy, friendly way. These values and ideas linger in the memory, to be dusted down and handled like precious stones. They may be looked at in wonder many times as children affirm and assimilate them for themselves.

Good storytelling engages children in a shared experience with the teller that can be deeply satisfying for everyone. This is especially evident if children are not just hearing the story but able to use their other senses, and interact with the teller and each other.

Where can I tell stories?

Almost anywhere! You may not be able to control which room you use for storytelling, but even the most unsuitable setting can be improved, upon reflection. The many strange places I have told stories include a ladies' cloakroom, a cupboard, a garden shed, a garage, a cow shed, and under a table. With an open invitation to use one's imagination, the most unlikely places can be made interesting, comfortable or exciting.

Think about the story you are going to tell. Where is it set? Where could it be set? Do you have to tell it in your usual meeting room? What interesting places do you have close by? Park, home, woodland, field, fire station, beach, farm, garden? If you plan to take children out, make sure you have parental consent, adequate clothing, sufficient cars and drivers if it's too far to walk, and plenty of proactive help. Resentful parents forced onto the rota will not be blessed or be a blessing by having not one but a profusion of progeny. Adolescent prima donnas escaping the adult meeting are not always a blessing, either! We all need to start our training somewhere, but an outdoor trip is not the best place. Be especially aware of dangers if you are going anywhere near water.

You may feel that all this is too much trouble for one short story. Why not create your story setting in your room? Tarpaulin covered with sand or gravel makes a great beach. Sacks of crunchy leaves in autumn and tipped onto the floor make a wonderful woodland setting. Leaves can also be used for other activities in your session, and children will enjoy sweeping them up afterwards. Creating settings will still mean thought, planning and work, but this can be delegated, and children will enjoy the enhanced story all the more.

If you are using a room, you will need to consider the following points:

Access to toilets

Ideally, you should be as close to the toilets as possible. You will have discovered that once small children have indicated their need for the toilet, there is very little or no time to waste. Make sure you have enough help for children to be whisked away without you having to suspend the story. You may feel it's not your responsibility, but check that there is toilet paper, soap and towels available, adding it to your list of things to bring, if necessary.

Room temperature

If the room is cold, think about additional heating, or using blankets as fun wraps for children. It may be helpful for children to warm up with an action rhyme or song before starting, and at intervals, if they have been sitting for a while. This has the additional advantage of diminishing wriggles.

If the room is too warm, open windows if you have them, provided that outside noise will not interfere with your story time. Alternatively, use fans to cool the room down. Provide small cool drinks.

Light

Lamps or spotlights can be added to brighten up a dark room. For a small group of children, you may wish to focus a lamp or spotlight on a particular area where you will be sitting. If you want to create a night-time or a quiet atmosphere, you can darken a window with paper or material, or draw curtains if you have them.

If the room is brightly lit with sunshine, think where the shade will be in the room at the time you tell your story, and prepare that area for children to sit. Shield children from full sun with curtains, material or screens.

Noise levels

Some rooms have concrete floors and bare walls, with low ceilings. These are not ideal for children, as the noise levels become tiring for all concerned and make concentration difficult. Think about carpeting the floor, not necessarily with new carpet. If funds are tight, ask around to discover people who are re-carpeting a room. Sample carpet squares can be bought cheaply. Each child can have their own named square to be their own special 'oasis.' Rugs and large cushions are helpful, too. Screens can be used to surround children, and help create a smaller setting.

If children use chairs, some hard flooring causes chairs to squeak loudly as they're moved around. Use large cushions or rugs instead.

Number of children

Make sure the room you use meets current health and safety standards for the number of children in the group. Always ensure that you have a correct ratio of adult helpers to children. If the room is too small for the number of children, action must be taken to find a larger room, possibly swapping with another group.

Comfort

Make the space you have as comfortable as possible. If the building you meet in belongs to the church, and you are able to use the same room on a regular basis, think creatively about how to make it an enjoyable experience to be there: carpet, large cushions, blankets, bean bags, curtains, room dividers or screens, pictures, posters, murals. Make a list of your regular activities and the playing space needed. Make a plan, allocating separate spaces for activities and playing space if possible, making the best use of the space available. Enlist help to decorate and furnish the room. Think child friendly, not adult.

If you are one of a number of users of the building you meet in, you will need to be more flexible. You probably already have several boxes that have to be kept at home or in other places and brought regularly, and the thought of adding extra items to bring is not attractive. However, you can help other people cultivate responsibility by allocating things for them to bring each time. Make it crystal clear what they should bring, where to bring it, and what time you need it. Initially, you may have to telephone and remind them. Next, you may have to tell them you are not going to telephone, but look forward to their arrival. Remember to praise and thank them for their efforts, and keep doing it.

Any textiles will need regular washing or cleaning. Again, this does not have to be your responsibility. Learn the art of delegation, with praise and thanksgiving!

Sharing a room

You may find yourself having to share a room with another group of children, leaders and helpers. This can be very distracting, and the best way to survive is to share as many activities as possible. This means a high degree of co-operation with other leaders when preparing sessions.

Stories for younger children can be shared with older children. The older ones may protest that they are beyond such baby stories. However, if they are encouraged to join in with younger children and help with actions and interactions, it's likely that they will thoroughly enjoy the experience. Also, it will help foster good relationships between different aged children.

How can I tell stories?

Learn the craft

Storytelling is a craft to be learned, but all storytellers had to begin at the beginning. If you are not familiar with children's stories, visit your local children's library to see what is available, and what children are looking at and reading today. This will help you pitch stories at the right level. Does your library have B-I-G books for small children? These are extra large books, usually kept on racks in the children's library, and are ideal for group storytelling. If your children's library doesn't have them, ask if they can use some of their budget to buy several.

Try to discern the difference between books that adults choose for children, and those children would choose for themselves.

- Practise reading stories aloud, to get used to the sound of your own voice. Then use a tape recorder and listen to yourself. Use this guide as a rough checklist to help you improve, giving yourself marks from 1–10, but don't be too hard on yourself.
  - When something funny happened, my voice chuckled.
  - When something sad happened, my voice was full of tears.
  - Sometimes I spoke quickly, and other times slowly, loudly, softly.
  - I changed my voice for different characters, and remembered which ones they were.
  - I changed the expression on my face for different feelings and characters.
  - Sometimes I paused to build suspense into the story.
  - I really enjoyed this story, and smiled a lot.

– I used my whole body to help tell the story.

- Choose a short, uncomplicated story (see What stories can I tell? on page 63), suiting it to the number of children in your group. It will increase your confidence if you are able to hold children's attention during the short time they are able to concentrate.

- If you intend to use your story to make a point, bear in mind that very young children will be unable to focus on more than one brief point.

- If possible, learn your story by heart, even when holding the book. If you are telling a made-up story, make brief headline notes to remind you what comes next. Work at making your story real to you; then it will be real to the children.

- Practise in front of a mirror, though you may want to choose a time when no one else is home! Make plenty of expressive faces, smile at yourself and relax. New storytellers are often concentrating so hard on remembering everything that they can have very fierce faces!

- As you practise your chosen story, don't rush. Use pauses to emphasise a point. A couple of seconds' silence can bring concentration back. Savour the sounds and effects of your voice and words. The human voice has an extensive range of sounds. Think what sounds you could add to your story.

- Allow plenty of time for telling your story, even though of itself it may be quite brief. Be ready for interruptions and distractions. Small children tend to go off at tangents when something you say reminds them of something else. If possible, weave everything into your story.

- Eye contact is important, as it involves children in the story with you. If you have a small group of children, sit with them, rather than facing them. You will have to work harder at eye contact and to show facial expressions, but it is possible. Make sure everyone can see and hear, including you! For a larger group, take the story as close as you can. It helps concentration and children feel included.
- Pray. Whether your story is a Bible story or a fictional one, pray that God will be present and that love will flow between you all as you tell your story.

Reinforcing the story

- Most children enjoy being read to, or told a story, and a well-told story, with plenty of vocal and body expression, and eye contact, is enough to sustain a short story, especially if the purpose of the story is just for pleasure and enjoyment. However, if we want children to actively remember a story or point, then reinforcing and participation is crucial. Children retain 60 per cent of what they do, 30 per cent of what they see and only 10 per cent of what they hear, but don't try and add too many ideas into one story. One or two may be plenty. Props and other media are not meant to detract from your story, or distract children. They are used to add another dimension, to help children take in what you are telling on other levels than just hearing, and to help them remember the point of the story.

- Pictures and posters are helpful, but bear in mind they will place an image in children's minds and may prevent them from developing their own pictures. We all know the disappointment of a film and its heroes not matching up to the picture in our heads when previously reading the story.

- Explain any difficult words or ideas before starting. Best of all, use different words, and simplify ideas!

- Don't be afraid to draw your own illustrations as you tell the story. These can be simple stick drawings that children can join in and draw with you. Small children are not looking for great works of art, and will appreciate your efforts.

- Mime can be a valuable tool when reading stories, but needs lots of mirror practice! Encourage children to join in with facial expressions and body movement – fear, surprise, joy, anger, sadness, etc.

- Use interaction to help keep children's interest. Ask questions: 'Why do you think he did that?' 'What do you think will happen next?' 'How did she feel?'

- It's helpful to tell children whether a story is true or made-up. Small children have difficulty telling the difference between Winnie the Pooh and Bible stories. If you are telling a Bible story but not using the Bible to read from, you can have an open Bible close by, to show children where your story comes from. Tell them that the story is true, even though it happened a long time ago. Pre-schoolers can't discern fact from fantasy, but to keep saying that this is a true story from the Bible will become embedded in their hearts when they do begin to distinguish truth from fiction, at around five or six years old. If you are using a parable-type story, you can say that this is not a true story, but there is truth in it.

- Use plenty of repetition of words and catchy phrases, inviting children to join in.
- Make up a simple rhyme for children to join in, with plenty of good sounds and actions or hand gestures.
- Chants can be used in the same way. Teach a chant phrase by phrase, and have children repeat it back to you, using the same rhythms and intonation. As the story progresses and you insert the chant, children will gradually learn it and join in with you.
- Echoing can be used to good effect, as an attention keeper. Prepare children to watch or listen for a given signal. Provide a simple line or two within the story every now and then, play your signal to invite children to echo it back to you.
- Children enjoy making and using sound effects with voices, bodies, instruments or everyday articles, e.g. telephone ringing, ambulance sirens, animal sounds, bangs and crashes, footsteps. These can be brought into the story at different times.
- These last five ways of involving children in the story can be pre-taught before you start. Show joyful antici-

pation by voice, face and gestures, as you get ready to repeat them together. Take a deep breath to invite them to get ready to join in.

- Simple puppets representing characters in the story can be helpful, e.g. faces drawn on craft sticks or round stickers, or fingers, paper plate puppets with a craft stick fixed to the back for holding, socks, paper bag. The puppets need to be given names and personalities, so that children can relate to them. These can be used just by you, or by the children, too.

- A conversation with a single puppet is an effective way of expressing thoughts and words children might not feel able or safe to express themselves. Sometimes, children can be frightened by large character puppets, so introduce them gently. Work on puppet skills, and practise often. Children's Ministry training days and conferences often include puppet workshops.

- Find props that will help tell your story, showing and using them at the right time in the story.

- Look at your story, and find several items that will help to tell it. Put these in a box or an apron with pockets, bringing them out at the right time. Alternatively, children can remove the items in advance and pass them around at the appropriate time in the story.

- Storytelling is often thought of only in terms of visual pictures or aural sounds, but we have other senses too that can be used to make stories more real and memorable. Touch, taste and smell should be added to sight and sound. Small children particularly enjoy and learn well through all their senses.

- **Touch.** Give children something to hold that connects with the story while it's being told, e.g. a shell, fir cone, paper tissue, elastic band, fur fabric. If your story is about sheep or shepherds, sit everyone on sheepskin rugs and make specific mention of stroking, touching and feeling the rug. If your story is about the sea, children can put bare feet on a layer of sand or gravel on tarpaulin, or hold a shell or dried seaweed.
- **Smell.** This is one of our most powerful senses. A long forgotten smell that is smelled many years later can bring back not just the actual event, but all the associated thoughts and feelings of that time. The sense of smell can help imprint a story on children's minds for all time. Investigate air sprays, gels, pot pourri, etc. to see if any of these could be used. If your story is set in a forest, spray forest air spray high in the air, letting it slowly drift down onto the children.
- **Taste.** Taste can boost imagination greatly. If your story is sad, let children taste salt water on individual teaspoons. They will recognise the taste of tears. Or have a box of tissues to pass around for children to wipe away pretend tears.

- When the story is finished, allow children to complete at their own pace. Don't rush on to the next thing. Some children may be ready to jump up and get going. Others may want to sit and dream, coming back to reality more slowly. Try yawning and stretching to encourage their return.

When can I tell stories?

- When children are hungry, they find it hard to concentrate. After food, they may be sleepy, or if your story has some energetic elements it's probably best to wait until their digestion has settled down. If you provide drinks for children, check the E numbers and sugar content, as these have dramatic effects on some children, and make quieter activities like storytelling difficult.
- If you have built up children's expectations, and they are waiting for someone or something exciting to happen, e.g. the entrance of a clown or the Easter bunny, they will be distracted and your story will suffer.
- Make sure children have been to the toilet and washed their hands before you begin.
- Don't overload children with too many stories. Make story time a special event, something to look forward to.
- If you wish to tell your story early in the session, allow children time to tell their news. Settle them with a calming poem or gentle action rhyme to encourage readiness to begin. If you use this regularly, children will recognise it and prepare themselves.
- A good time to tell a story is after activity or an ener-

getic game, but if they are too restless or hyped up from the game, calm them down with your calming poem, or gentle action rhyme, before beginning.

- If you leave your story until near the end of your session, children may be tired and hungry. You may have to rush it as time runs out. Parents may start arriving to collect children, and your story will be lost.

What stories can I tell?

Bible stories

Choose subjects and topics that are appropriate to the children in your group. Convey the truth, but use broad brush strokes rather than deep detail, as children are at the very beginning of a long journey of learning and faith. Bible stories will gradually build a library in their minds and hearts. The stories can stand alone, or you can bring out one spiritual concept or idea for children to focus on, and find practical ways for children to apply it.

Bible stories can be told in your own words, using ideas from the previous section and a brightly coloured, illustrated children's Bible. Be careful not to add your own ideas or interpretation to the story, either in background information or content. Use Jesus the Storyteller as your role model (see chapter 3).

Alternatively, there are many books of Bible stories written for children. Investigate these carefully, as some are better than others. The Children's Ministry teaching programme provides a Bible story, told in an age-appropriate way, in every session.

Be enthusiastic about the story, and enjoy it. Children will copy you. What view of the Bible are children forming if your presentation is dull and uninteresting?

Made-up stories

Even if you think you have little imagination, you may well be surprised at the wealth of ideas, plots and characters inside your head just waiting to be used.

- Draw on your own and your family's experiences, funny and serious, and bits and pieces of remembered stories from your childhood.
- Read and listen to children's stories, to see how they're crafted and what children enjoy.
- Don't try to be complicated or clever. Keep it simple.
- Don't set your story in a complicated context. Very young children don't yet understand concepts of time or space.
- Practise your story in the bath, in the shower, in the car (keep watching the traffic), in front of a mirror (but not the rear-view mirror).
- Try your story out on your own or someone else's children. Young children usually give an immediate and undisguised reaction, and you will quickly tell how good your story is.
- If your story goes down well, do it! Whatever happens, don't give up. Keep trying!

Fiction story and picture books

Most of us remember books and stories from our childhood. Some of them, while loved by us, may not be suitable today. Older children can benefit from the prose and poetry of those stories, but younger children will enjoy the ones that have been brought up to date for today's generation. Ladybird has a very good range of both classical and new stories in bright, colourful format.

However well you think you know children's fiction books, make time to check out your local children's library, school classrooms and libraries, and the bookshelves of families with young children. Ask, listen and learn what children are enjoying today. It's not possible in this book to give a definitive list of good children's literature, but to help you get started, the following books or series are worth a look:

Bible story and other Christian books

- *Jesus the Friend* (Ladybird)
- *Jesus the Helper* (Ladybird)
- *When the World was New* (Lion)
- *God's Quiet Things* (Lion)
- *I Wonder Why* (Lion)
- *The Minstrel's Tale* (Lion)
- *The Goodbye Boat* (Lion)
- *The Tale of Three Trees* (Lion)
- *Henry's Song* (Lion)

- *Who Made Me?* (Lion)
- *The Very Worried Sparrow* (Lion)

Non-Christian fiction

- *Percy the Park Keeper*, Nick Butterworth (Picture Lions), and other Nick Butterworth books
- *Mog the Cat*, Judith Kerr (Collins), and other Mog books
- *The Tiger Who Came to Tea*, Judith Kerry (Picture Lions)
- *We're Going on a Bear Hunt*, Michael Rosen and Helen Oxenbury (Walker Books)
- *The Last Train*, Kim Lewis (Walker Books), and other Kim Lewis books
- *You'll Soon Grow into Them*, Pat Hutchins (Red Fox), and other Pat Hutchins books
- *A Boy Wants a Dinosaur*, Satoshi Kitamura and Hiawyn Oram (Andersen Press)
- *Tractor and Digger Save the Day*, Jim Eldridge and David Melling (Bloomsbury Paperbacks)
- *Peace at Last*, *Five Minutes' Peace* and *All in One Piece*, Jill Murphy (Walker Books)
- *Alfie and Annie Rose Storybook*, Shirley Hughes (Red Fox)
- *Tales of Trotter Street*, Shirley Hughes (Walker Books)
- *Old Bear* stories by Jane Hissey (Red Fox)

Don't be afraid of repetition. Children love to hear the same stories, especially if they are well told. They notice all omissions of familiar words, and will want to join in words and phrases with you. They wait with anticipation for any scary bits, and because they know what happens in the end, they are reassured that it will work out fine.

5. Storytelling with Five- to Nine-year-olds

Why should I tell stories?

Look at chapter 1 again for reasons to tell stories to children. Good storytelling is a precious gift that the teller gives to listeners, but the storyteller also receives many gifts in return. These make storytelling very worthwhile. As the storyteller, you receive:

- respect for your knowledge, skill and authority
- an opportunity to influence others for good
- affirmation
- pleasure in being listened to
- pleasure as you watch children's faces and see the story working
- pleasure in performing well with language, and different ways of presentation
- satisfaction in creating, assessing, gathering children

into your story, with feedback and reinforcement
- release from the usual constraints of teacher or leader, and a different relationship with children, perhaps more playful or relaxed
- acceptance as part of the group
- an opportunity to discover your own feelings
- attention.

Where can I tell stories?

Stories can be told in almost any place. Your story may give a clue as to its natural setting or occasion. If so, try to provide it. Some of the suggestions given here mean going out on location, and rely on parental consent, extra helpers, a vivid imagination and advance planning. Some of the suggestions can be created in a room or building:

- top of a bus
- garden
- beach
- museum
- barbecue
- camp(fire)
- story walk
- park
- sports centre
- corridor
- tent (home-made or bona fide)
- train

- outdoor/indoor picnic site
- donkey sanctuary
- kitchen
- farm
- darkened room
- zoo
- McDonalds.

Stories that have other effects, puppets, or props, may not need a scene set for them, and can be contained in the room you normally use. Take a good look at the room, and think how it can be improved to make it more story-friendly. Why should we make this extra effort to make a place story-friendly? Don't we have enough to prepare and do? Why should we go to so much trouble for what is just a small part of our session together?

For thousands of years, as people have been captivated by stories and storytellers, they have experienced warmth and comfort, not just from their fires, but from the whole enfolding experience of being together, and exploring the world and their ideas from a safe place. We rarely build fires and sit around them to tell our tales, but we do have the means to provide warmth and a degree of comfort that will add that extra dimension to our togetherness in the story. For some children, this corporate embrace and iden-tity allows them an escape and acceptance that is not theirs in reality, and we should do all we can to foster such opportunities.

Factors to take into consideration:

- If the room is used for other purposes, e.g. classroom, community use, storage of boxes, and you are not the sole user, you may need to think of portable ways to make a story setting. These need not be elaborate, nor do they have to be your sole responsibility. Decide with your helpers what is needed, and delegate. Children can be asked to help set up the story area whenever you need to use it. This will help them own it.

- If you are the sole user of the room, is there space to set up a permanent story area? If so, what would make it attractive and comfortable for the children in your group? Ask them for their ideas.

  - Suggestions – carpet, rugs, large cushions, bean bags, low chairs, small tables, screens, bookshelves with up-to-date books, both Bible stories, Christian and non-Christian fiction.

  - If the budget is tight, enlist a small team (not necessarily children's workers) to find out who has spare rugs or cushions to give. The team can investigate local markets and cheap fabric shops, and find bright, colourful material to recover if necessary.

  - Children can make posters regularly so that the area continues to look interesting and different.

  - Check out books that interest the children, and look in your local children's library, schools and Christian bookshop. Compile a book list and ask each family in the church to buy one book a month/quarter for the story area.

- As children arrive, wait to leave or during spare moments in the programme, encourage them to sit, look and read. Have a helper watch for particular children who may need a safe haven or a quiet place just to be. If children want to borrow books, make sure a list is kept, and that they are returned.
- If the room you use isn't big enough, think laterally. Where else could you tell stories in the building you use? Can you swap with a smaller group who use a larger room? Can you use the end of a corridor? What about the foyer? Weather permitting, do you need to be indoors to tell your story? Is there a large porch away from roads that you could use? Car parks are not the safest places for children, but do you have trees and grass around the building you meet in? Does anyone from the church live nearby, and have a garden, or a shed?

How can I tell stories?

Learn the craft

The props or media we use to tell the story may differ for older children, but the craft of learning how to tell a story remains essentially the same for all children. There are no short cuts to becoming a good storyteller, who can hold children's attention and create the miraculous giving and receiving that a well-told story brings for teller and listeners.

You may not feel that storytelling comes naturally to

you, and the thought of learning this craft is daunting, especially when there is so much else to do. Let me encourage you to begin, and continue until you succeed. Almost everyone has stories within, from their own experiences or those of others, and the urge to tell them. Almost everyone can find a children's fiction story they enjoy. Almost everyone can read it, make it their own and share it. Everyone will find the Bible crammed with the best stories! Adventure, danger, goodies, baddies, conflict, tension, suspense, drama . . .

- Practise reading stories aloud to get used to the sound of your own voice. Then use a tape recorder and listen to yourself. Use this guide as a rough checklist to help you improve, giving yourself marks from 1–10, but don't be too hard on yourself.
  - When something funny happened, my voice chuckled.
  - When something sad happened, my voice was full of tears.
  - Sometimes I spoke quickly, and other times slowly, loudly, softly.
  - I changed my voice for different characters, and remembered which ones they were.
  - I changed the expression on my face for different feelings and characters.
  - Sometimes I paused to build suspense into the story.
  - I really enjoyed this story, and smiled a lot.

- – I used my whole body to help tell the story.
- Know your listeners well. Choose a short, uncomplicated story (see What stories can I tell? on page 85), suiting it to the number of children in your group. Make sure the story is appropriate to their age and understanding. If you have a wide age range of children, aim for somewhere in the middle-to-younger children. Most older children will cope well, especially if occasionally you lift a story to their level and draw younger children along with you with props or special effects. Alternatively, you could tell a story for children within a narrower age band while others are busy with another activity.
- Whether your chosen story is to be read or told from memory, allow it to lie fallow in your mind. Turn it over from time to time, while you decide what to include and what to leave out. Visualise the story. If it becomes real to you, it will be real to the children. Knowing it well will give you confidence to communicate in non-verbal ways with your eyes, face, body and emotions. Decide what extras, if any, you will use to reinforce your story. Hold your book or Bible, even though you may not read the story directly from it. If you are telling a made-up story, make brief headline notes on a small card to remind you what comes next.
- Practise in front of a mirror at home. Watch your facial expressions, gestures and body language. Smile at yourself often, and relax. Don't rush your story. If you leave something vital out, don't be afraid to say: 'I

75

forgot to tell you a most important thing . . .' and briefly recap. Use pauses to emphasise a point, or build tension. A couple of seconds' silence can help bring concentration back.

- Savour the sounds and effects of your voice and words. Listen to the rhythm of your words. Try using alliteration – when all words start with or share the same sound, e.g. sing a song of sixpence – and onomatopoeia – when words sound like what they do or are, e.g. cuckoo, sizzle, bang. Children enjoy hearing language used in this way, and you can make up alliterative or onomatopoeic phrases for them to join in. The human voice has an extensive range of sounds. Think what sounds could be added to your story. Repetition and exaggeration are useful tools, too.

- Allow plenty of time for telling your story, even though of itself it may be quite short. This is especially important if you intend using interaction to help keep concentration and reinforce the story.

- Eye contact is vital. Next to your voice, your eyes are the most important means of communication. Let your eyes rest on one individual for a few seconds, and then move on to another. Don't just focus in one direction. Eye contact draws children into the story, and you can tell who is with you. Make sure everyone can see and hear, including you! Take the story as close as you can without any barriers between you. It helps concentration, and children feel included. Don't be afraid to move around, taking children's focus with you. Get in their faces. Pour yourself into the story and into them.

- Once children have been at school for a while, their attention span is likely to be longer, and a ten to fifteen minute story should be possible. However, in any group you will nearly always have at least one child who cannot concentrate for very long. If you make your story to fit their attention span, it may leave others wanting more and dissatisfied.

  Try to involve the restless child in your story: handing round props, picking up discarded items, preparing things to show, etc. If other children are enjoying the story, you may find eventually that the restless child is listening, even though they may be doing something else. As a last resort, you can have a helper ready to do something else quietly with the child until the story is finished. If you have a child like this in your group, try to make sure they have some busy activity just before the story, to help release pent-up energy, but be careful not to hype them up too much as this will have the opposite effect. Afterwards, praise children for listening well and give opportunity for action.

- It's helpful to begin your story with an introduction, to focus children's attention and invite them into your story. Some may come reluctantly and need to be drawn in. 'Do you know what happened when. . .?' 'Have you ever had a day when. . .?' 'Did I ever tell you about. . .?' 'When I was seven years old. . .' Share an experience from your childhood, not necessarily good, that they will relate to, and that has some relevance to your story. Arouse their curiosity and anticipation, but don't get carried away with the introduction and run out of time to tell the story.

- You can choose to begin your story part way through, at an interesting or exciting point, and then return to the beginning – e.g. describing Joseph stuck down an empty well: 'How did he get there?'

- Set the scene for your story, particularly if dealing with unfamiliar Bible places, customs, etc. You can use maps or pictures to help. Keep Bible stories in their original culture and setting, but don't get bogged down in too much detail or explanation. Allow children to work things out for themselves. You can ask them to close their eyes and imagine how it might have been.

- Be prepared with ideas to boost flagging attention. These could be from your range of props, or a puppet who makes an intermittent appearance, a repetitive phrase or rhyme, a gesture, sound effects, a joke, a change of pace, mood or voice. You can work in an interruption from a helper or child, primed beforehand, or have someone make an unexpected entrance in costume.

- Stop when you've finished. Don't dribble on, or think you have to tie up all loose ends. Some stories are told just for enjoyment. Maybe the Holy Spirit needs to work, or children need to think for themselves what the story means. If you aim to make one point, like Jesus, our model storyteller, work at summarising your point during preparation. Don't bash children over the head with it at the end, but find ways to deliver it simply and directly in just as exciting or dramatic ways as part of the story, while children are still listening. It can sometimes be helpful to give a brief, personal application, before returning to the story. Alternatively, ask questions during or after the story that will help children find the point and work things out for themselves.

- Expect to fail sometimes. You're human, and so are the children. Don't take storytelling or yourself so seriously that it becomes a bruising disaster if the story falls apart, or you don't deliver it in the way you've prepared.

- Pray. Whether your story is a Bible story or a fictional one, pray that God will be present, and that love will flow between you all as you tell your story.

- If you are telling a Bible story, and want to make a point or application, let the spiritual lesson penetrate your own life first so that you can communicate it personally and effectively, with excitement. Ask God to prepare your own heart and those of your listeners. Expect him to answer!

Reinforcing the story

- Most children enjoy listening to stories. A well-told story with plenty of verbal and non-verbal expression is enough to sustain a short story or part of a serial, especially if the purpose of the story is just for pleasure and enjoyment. But if children are required to remember a story or point, then reinforcing and participation is crucial. Children retain 60 per cent of what they do, 30 per cent of what they see and only 10 per cent of what they hear. However, too many props and other media can detract from your story, or distract children. They are there to add another dimension, other than just hearing, and help children remember the point of the story.

- Think about incorporating jokes or riddles.
- Short songs, rhymes, catchy, alliterative or onomatopoeic phrases can be used at intervals throughout the story. Tell children when you are about to start them, giving a key word or gesture as a signal, or count them in. These can be taught before the start of your story, or written out for them to read or sing together.
- Visual aids can be helpful, including pictures, posters, objects, flannelgraph or teazlegraph. Give children flannelgraph or teazlegraph pieces in advance, and invite them to add them to the board at the right time. Have a helper take responsibility for assembling the flannelgraph.
- Children enjoy seeing a story develop as it's being told. Make a freeze-frame frieze and illustrate your story as you tell it, using stick figures with simple backgrounds in each freeze-frame. Alternatively, different children can be responsible for each freeze-frame, or ask someone more artistically talented to help create the story with you. Go through the story with them beforehand.

- Another idea for story development is to use origami or moulding balloons. You don't have to be expert at all these things. Ask around. People may surprise you with their talents. (Can you rise to the challenge of incorporating into your story someone who plays the spoons?) Prepare the story with them beforehand.

- Use a character from the story dressed in costume, who will tell what happened from their point of view.

- Use puppets. It's hard to sustain long narrative with a puppet, but a single puppet can ask questions, or interject with things children might think but not say out loud. Puppets can ask children what they think should be done to resolve a situation. Effective puppetry needs a great deal of practise. It can be hard to manage your story and work the puppet at the same time, so enlist help. Keep dialogue and actions simple.

- Set up a trail or treasure hunt story for small groups of children. Begin the story with the whole group, and give the first clue. As each group moves on to solve the clue, they can find another piece of the story with another clue for someone to read to their group. This makes a good outdoor story activity for summer.

- Consider telling the story briefly, and have children act it out afterwards, with or without dressing up. Think what simple props might help.

- Investigate videos to tell or reinforce your story. Video clips can kick-start role-play, where children take the part of different characters in a story and act out what they would do.

- Use 'action' stories, where the audience responds with a noise/action on every occurrence of certain words or phrases. These can be taught before the story begins.
- Lay out a number of key objects at the beginning of the story and pass them round at the right time. Alternatively, hide the objects around your meeting place. Stop the story, and ask what is needed next. Send a volunteer to search for it while everyone counts, before continuing with the story.
- Write out sentences, phrases or brief dialogue for characters beforehand. Number them, and give them out at the start of the story. Cue children in at the right time with a signal or sound.
- Have a collection of hats or dressing up clothes for different characters. Choose individual children to wear these as the character, putting them on and taking them off as the character moves in and out of the story. Alternatively, use a helper to wear all the hats at different times, taking on all the characters as you tell the story.
- Be prepared that occasionally children may be so caught up in the story that your careful preparation of props or other media may become irrelevant. That would be great!

When can I tell stories?

- You may decide that it's very important to include a Bible story in each session, so that children hear Bible truth on a regular basis, build up their knowledge and are helped to apply a particular teaching point to their lives. Plan with your leaders and helpers, looking carefully at the teaching material you use. Find different ways of presenting the Bible story each time, so that children will not become bored with the same methods.

- The Children's Ministry Teaching Programme uses a four-step plan and the Bible story is always included in Step 2, as the central point of the session, with other activities leading to it or resulting from it. Methods of telling the Bible story with the Children's Ministry Teaching Programme vary, and this should be enough to keep children interested. Most children enjoy the security and anticipation of knowing what is coming next; however, some children may become disinterested if stories are told at a predictable time. You can't please all children all the time, any more than you can please all adults all the time. You will probably make a decision based on what suits the majority of children in your group. Make special efforts to involve and include children who may find your decision difficult.

- Other stories are sometimes included in the Children's Ministry Teaching Programme, often on the Resource CD, and children are usually invited to do something active with their hands while the story is being told. This use of story is often to lead into the Bible story, or to provide an opportunity to discuss and share what children think, in preparation for the Bible story.

- If you decide to begin the session with a story, give

children time to settle first, and introduce your story or character.

- The end of a Sunday morning session is not usually the best time for storytelling. Some churches have a fairly flexible ending time, and you may find your story has finished, but the adult service has not. Other churches have a tighter schedule, with children returning to the main service at a set time. This can sometimes mean a rushed story, or the inability to finish it before children need to leave.

- Children who are hungry or restless don't make good listeners. If necessary, feed and water them, and give opportunities to expend excess energy before story time.

- Storytelling of all kinds makes an ideal addition to programmes for kids clubs, uniformed groups, after school clubs, child minding, etc. Make story time something to look forward to, as a special treat. Give children time to wind down after other activities. Encourage them to prepare to listen and become involved in the story-making process. Place your story in the programme where there is plenty of time for it, with no need to rush.

- If you plan to tell a serial story, it can be helpful to make this a special and set time in the programme for children to anticipate and look forward to. Once a serial is begun, make sure you tell it regularly and finish it, or children will be disappointed and may decide not to get involved next time. If using a serial story during a holiday club, or a setting where children are meeting every day for a few days, a cliff-hanger ending to each part of the story, helps to keep everyone interested.

What stories can I tell?

Bible stories

Choose subjects and topics appropriate to the children in your group. Some Old Testament stories can be gruesome, and need not have every detail spelled out, nor should we be ultra sensitive and make all Bible stories saccharine sweet. This doesn't give a true perspective of Scripture, people's lives, or help children learn how God works.

It's important to use Old and New Testament Bible stories, to give a good overall perspective of God at work in and through people's lives. These can include creation, the patriarchs, Old Testament characters, prophets and kings, the life and teaching of Jesus, the beginning and spread of the church, and God's ultimate plan to have a people for the praise of his glory eternally.

The Children's Ministry Teaching Programme has a four-year cycle for the 5–9s age group, covering these topics and more. The Bible stories are clearly set in their own times and culture, yet presented in ways children of this generation can understand. Of course, Bible stories can be told in your own words, using ideas from the previous section. Be careful, when using your own words and imagination to tell Bible stories, that you don't alter the story. Alternatively, you can choose to read your story from one of the many books of Bible stories available for children.

Don't just choose familiar stories, but look for unfamiliar stories or characters. There are a number of people whose lives we don't know a great deal about, and who only get a brief mention in the Bible. Make a variety of approaches. Be a mouse in the corner; create a dialogue with a stranger passing through after the event and asking questions of a person who was there; tell the story from a child's perspective.

Made-up stories

Children love to hear a well told made-up story, especially if it's from your own experience. Most of us have a wealth of ideas and characters gleaned from our childhood and schooldays, family life and history, knowledge of people, funny or sad things that have happened, snippets of information that can be woven into stories, and half-remembered stories from when we were young.

Give children the opportunity to tell a made-up story in the round. Prepare an introduction and a beginning to set the story in motion. You don't have to think of an ending. Explain what is going to happen, and begin. Finish your part of the story with a cliff-hanger sentence e.g: 'Just as they were beginning to settle down for the night, a bright light flashed through the window . . .' The story continues around the group, with everyone participating and leaving their part of the story open for the next person to carry on. These stories can take on a life of their own, as no one knows where they will go. Such stories don't need controlling, but may need some guidance and encouragement. If children are stuck, ask questions to provoke them to think what might happen next. This kind of story gives children an understanding of how to tell stories, and a greater appreciation of your efforts.

Fiction stories

Some of the stories we remember from our childhood may not be written in a way that children are used to hearing or reading today. Many of the classic tales have been re-written for today's children, and make suitable reading with and to groups of children as serials. Some, like Ladybird classics, have been abbreviated and can be read at one sitting.

Make time to check out your local children's library, school libraries, classrooms and bookshelves of families with children in this age range. Most children's libraries carry larger picture books, with stories for older readers and listeners. These can be helpful for group reading or telling.

Ask the children in your group what kind of books they enjoy reading or having read to them. The following very brief list of books or series might be worth looking at:

Christian fiction

- *Shoelaces and Brussels Sprouts*, Nancy Simpson (Chariot Victor), and others in the Alex Series.

- *The Merchant and the Thief*, Ravi Zacharias (Chariot Victor)
- *Adam Racoon Parables for Kids Series*, Glen Keane (Chariot Victor)
- John Bunyan's *Pilgrim's Progress* retold by Geraldine McCaughrean (Hodder Christian Books)
- *Angels, angels all around*, Bob Hartman (Lion)
- *Anna Magdalena*, Kay Kinnear (Lion)
- *Beggars, Beasts and Easter Fire*, Carol Green (Lion)
- *The Christmas Play*, Claire Bevan and Julie Park (Lion)
- *50 Five-Minute Stories*, Lynda Neilands (Children's Ministry)
- *50 Stories for Special Occasions*, Lynda Neilands (Children's Ministry)

Non-Christian fiction

- *Justin and the Big Fight*, Bernard Ashley (Puffin)
- *Jake Again*, Annette Butterworth (Hodder StoryBook)
- *Invisible Stanley*, Jeff Brown (Mammoth)
- *The Angel of Nitshill Road*, Anne Fine (Mammoth)
- *Sparks: Historical Adventures* (Franklin Watts). Stories about children written in the different historical settings of ancient Greece, times of invaders and settlers, Tudors and Stuarts, the Victorian era and twentieth-century history, e.g. *Dr Barnardo's Boys*, Karen Wallace.
- *Deep Trouble*, Lynne Markham (Mammoth)
- *The Aardvark who Wasn't Sure*, Jill Tomlinson (Mammoth)
- *The Borrowers*, Mary Norton (J.M. Dent & Sons)

- Picture storybooks for older children: *The Witness*, Robert Westall (Macmillan) and *Weslandia*, Paul Fleischman (Walker Books)

Children in the upper ranges of the 5–9s age group may well be reading, or want to read, the Harry Potter books by J.K. Rowling. Adults, too, have discovered that Harry Potter is a cross-over market, and the books are also published in adult covers as well as those for children. The film of the first book, the resultant spin-offs and school projects make it difficult for any child to be unaware of Harry Potter, or to remain uninvolved.

There has been, and still is, a great deal of controversy among Christians about the suitability of these books for children in Christian families. If you are leading, teaching, helping, or caring for children in any capacity, then you need to read the series so far to make your own conclusions and to guide the children in your care. Also strongly recommended is John Houghton's book, *A Closer Look at Harry Potter* (Kingsway). As a writer of fantasy himself, John Houghton gives a timely and valuable insight into the whole subject. He believes that because of their content and structure, Harry Potter books are not suitable for children under ten years of age, and that children who are highly impressionable should be even older before reading them.

6. Storytelling with Nine-year-olds and Over

Why should I tell stories?

Stories are probably less often read with and to children over the age of nine. As they develop their own interests and friends, it becomes harder for parents to find the time and place to read to their children. Most parents will have had the experience of buying a 'suitable' book for an older child, only to find that it remains unread. Children of this age are beginning the long journey of separation from their parents' ideas and choices, and are searching for their own. To read or not to read, to listen or not to listen may seem a small stand to make, but is a step along the tricky road to adult independence. However, there may be times of a child's choosing when they will be happy to find an oasis of easier or less turbulent space than the present, and have someone read to or with them. Wise parents will understand and support their child's choices, while seeking to guide them through prayer and discussion.

It's also easier to suppose that if children wish to read, then they can choose their own books and get on with it. Reading alone is one of life's greatest pleasures, but many children today don't read well enough to read a whole book by themselves, or are distracted by so many other things that are easier, quicker and perceived to be more fun to do. For parents and teachers, one of the greatest pluses for the *Harry Potter* books is that even children who have not read alone or well, are managing to read and enjoy six hundred pages, and clamouring for more. This makes the whole debate about their suitability even more difficult. Generally speaking, most children are reading fewer books today than in previous generations, apart from set school books. Lengthy study and analysis of set books are not usually the best ways to encourage children to enjoy reading for pleasure.

It's important for parents to know their child's interests. They can make some initial, quiet investigations on their child's behalf, looking for magazines, helpful websites, newspaper articles, TV and radio programmes, videos, museums, galleries, concerts, special events. In fact, anything that is legitimate and will not harm children can be used to stimulate a child to explore, research and have fun learning about their chosen subject, whether it's pop stars or snail keeping. If parents show encouragement and excitement, without sighing criticism, offering help with reading, writing letters, building a collection, storyboard, scrap book, etc., they may be invited to tag along for some parts of the journey. This may not be the reading of stories together in the manner of former years, but can help build important bridges of communication and bond the parent/child relationship in new and lasting ways.

Leaders and teachers in a church setting need to be aware that, conscious of peer pressure and the growing need to leave perceived childlike ways behind, it may not be considered cool to have stories read in a group setting. However, the reasons for storytelling given in chapter 1 apply to everyone, not just young children and adults. Storytelling undoubtedly has great advantages for children in this age group, as they test their boundaries and become increasingly aware of some of the realities of adulthood. It's the methods of storytelling that need to change, not the storytelling itself.

Where can I tell stories?

If you have read previous chapters, it will be clear that stories can be told in almost any place, and this applies especially to older children, who can more easily be taken to other locations, apart from a church building. Adequate safety provision, thought and planning still need to be employed. Children themselves can be involved in all the preliminary practical preparation, but the occasional complete surprise is great fun.

When you have decided what story you wish to tell, then you need to apply some imagination to think of an appropriate or fun setting for it. This obviously depends on what is available in your area, but with ingenuity and determination it's possible to think of different scene-setting ideas. If you feel inadequate or too inexperienced to tackle this, unearth a small team of creative people. They don't necessarily have to be children's workers or part of your current team. Tell them your idea for a story, and let them brainstorm ideas for it. Don't forget to include the children themselves in this process. They are more likely to own the story, enjoy it and remember it if they have been involved in its set up.

Some of the ideas for story locations given for younger age groups will apply to nine-year-olds and over. Several additional locations that you may not have considered, and whose purpose is explained below in 'What story styles can I use?' (see page 97), are:

- cellar
- swimming-pool
- farm barn
- bus stop
- chip shop
- cemetery
- sweet or chocolate factory.

Of course, a story can also be told and contained within a room or building, but you may still need to consider a setting for it. If this is not appropriate because of time, space, cost, transport, etc., précis your story into different sections. When the story has been completed in whatever form you use, allocate each section to a small group. Groups can use their imaginations to give location, colour, sounds, background music, light or shade for their section of the story. Bring them all together to read their précis aloud, in order, and offer their different contributions.

How can I tell stories?

Learn the craft

The format of storytelling may seem to be entirely different for older children, but many of the principles outlined in 'Learning the craft' for 3–5s and 5–9s also apply to children aged nine plus. Obviously, your presentation styles will be age appropriate, but you will still need to:

- know your listeners well, considering their ages and abilities
- learn to tell a good joke or riddle
- practise verbal and non-verbal skills, to communicate effectively
- know your chosen story well, preparing and practising it, whatever form it takes
- learn to laugh at your own prattfalls and not take yourself too seriously
- learn to use the minimum number of words with the maximum impact
- use a broad range of language skills, to increase children's enjoyment of the story
- be relaxed

- allow plenty of time for your story
- make and maintain good eye contact and expression
- be aware of children who, for whatever reason, find it difficult to join in, and look for ways to involve them
- be encouraging
- be ready to explain briefly any obscure names, terms or customs
- sometimes ask questions to bring out a point
- sometimes invite a response.

A large proportion of the craft of storytelling depends upon the relationship you have with the children in your group, and the good control you are able to exercise, without domination or manipulation. The measure of relationship and control will determine to a large extent how much influence and teaching you are able to impart through the medium of storytelling. Relationship and control are important right across the age range, but particularly so for nine-year-olds and over. If you have not previously developed and fostered these, it may be hard to start, but very worthwhile.

- Begin by looking for things that interest individual children, and ask questions to find out more.
- Listen carefully to their responses and ask more questions. Some older children in a group setting may not initially respond well, as they don't necessarily want to show their desire for inclusion or relationship in front of their friends. Don't give up, but take any natural

opportunities to cultivate friendship and relationship when they are less threatened by the pack.

- Look out for children at times when you are not directly responsible for them. Some will be happy to acknowledge you, but others may seem disinterested. Don't be discouraged. Remember what you were like at their age.
- Be friendly and encouraging, without hassle.
- Follow up strugglers and stragglers with kindness and concern.
- Be as honest and open as you can about your own life and interests, sharing mistakes and ideas as appropriate, without preaching.
- During the time when you are responsible for the children in your group, learn how to have fun and still keep control.
- Practise fairness and discipline according to the rules and guidelines known and agreed by all. Try to include all children, without fear or favouritism.
- Pray, and ask God to help you love and take a real interest in the children in your group.
- If making relationships and keeping control in the right way prove to be more than just a challenge, acknowledge that you may need help and training, and actively seek it out.

What story styles can I use?

Children of this age still need stories to be reinforced, and to be able to participate in the storytelling experience. If you are using a Bible story, it becomes increasingly important for them to remember not only the story, but the application for their lives. Non-Bible stories can also have a good and lasting influence on children.

When you have chosen your story, whether it's a Bible story, a made-up or fiction story, and thought of an appropriate or fun setting for it, you will need to consider its style of telling. There must be thousands of story styles, and you will have your own favourites.

- Depending on the ages and abilities of the children in your group, you may find that some of the ideas for 5–9s will be appropriate, and can be used effectively. Older children usually need a greater degree of participation and involvement, unless the story is brief or particularly appropriate for them, e.g. someone of their own age whom they know, or a topic that is particularly important to them at that time.

- Tell your chosen story briefly to the whole group, emphasising the characters involved. Divide the characters between different groups of children. Each group can discuss their character's nature, personality, motives and what they said and did. Groups can elect that character from among them. A leader or helper begins the story, and conducts its progress as each character acts out their part. This kind of story works best without too many breaks, but with careful leadership it can be stopped and restarted as children think out and rework their parts. In taking on different characters, children are able to discern what made them behave in the way that they did. Less confident children are able to participate in the discussion and ideas process within the group, without needing to take a leading role on this occasion.

- Some stories, even Bible stories, can be written in a murder/mystery style. If you don't think you have the necessary skills to do this, there are others who probably have. Seek them out in plenty of time, and work together on creating your story and characters. You can use a murder mystery game as your model. Explain to children how the story works, and that it is the job of the detective to discover the murderer. If preferred, adults can act out the story while children watch. If you use this method, have the detective ask children questions as the story develops, and use them to help in the discovery process. Write the story concisely, so that it need not take up the whole of your programme. Dressing up is an option to be considered.

- Visit a local cemetery where there are ancient head-stones. Children can write down names of the long-departed occupants, dates, and any inscriptions. Later, in small groups with helpers, or as a whole group, encourage children to make up a life story for the person they chose. It will help if you have one you prepared earlier to show how it's done. Don't use this idea if you have grieving children in the group. However, it need not be a morbid experience, but an opportunity to talk about death, death of pets or people, or to think about Bible characters who didn't die (Enoch and Elijah), or the story of Jesus and Lazarus (John 11:1–44), or the resurrection of Jesus from death. Prepare yourself and your helpers to be ready to answer questions. A useful book for this topic is, *Will My Rabbit Go to Heaven?* by Jeremie Hughes (Lion).

- Children can take turns to use a PS2 or computer game. Discuss characters beforehand, and possible scenarios. Children waiting for a turn can comment on what is happening, what the characters are feeling, and make up a story around it. Try to involve everyone as the story progresses. This can be just a fun activity, but if you wish to make a point or application it is often possible to draw one out. Make it short and appropriate to the children.

- There are some children who have remarkable skills to create their own computer games. Source them with a story idea or outline, and let them devise a game around it. If required, work out an application with the creator. When completed, they can show and play it with others in the group.

- Play on video part of an old film that no one will have seen. Name the characters in the film. Turn down the sound. Everyone can contribute ideas or guesses as to what is happening in the story. Alternatively, nominate helpers to take the parts of the characters. Afterwards, turn up the volume for children to hear the original idea.

- A similar idea can be used for watching part of a video of a football match or other sport. Turn down the sound and choose two commentators with microphones to give a running commentary of the game.

- Your chosen story can be performed by puppet theatre. This idea can become a larger activity over several sessions, with children making the puppets and the theatre. You may need extra help to teach children new skills to create puppets, backdrops, stage, curtains, lighting, sound effects, music, lyrics for songs, speeches for characters, etc. Aim to make it an activity that everyone can join in. The enjoyment is often as much in the creation of the theatre and the puppets as the production itself. Think about performing the story for a younger or older age group.

- You may be able to find a video of your chosen story. Time and the purpose of your meeting will decide whether it can be shown at one sitting, or in serial form.

- Some Bible stories could be told in a cellar, cave or darkened room for atmosphere, e.g. David hiding from Saul, the birth of Jesus, or stories of early Christians taking refuge from persecution in the catacombs in Rome. You might encourage children to make murals or paintings for walls, to describe how characters felt, or tell what they wanted to say. Use the opportunity to discuss graffiti – art form or vandalism?

- Organise the use of a farm barn to tell the story of Gideon, a young man called to lead God's people from the clutches of the Midianites (Judges 6). Have a Christian farmer explain or demonstrate the normal Bible times procedure for threshing wheat. Use the opportunity to discuss tough times, fear, God's call. The farmer can tell a brief, funny story, or one that tells of God's help in crisis from his own experience. Any chance of a tractor ride (under more than adequate supervision of course!)?

- Occasionally, you may find yourself out and about in a busy place with a small group of children e.g. shopping mall, market, airport, bus station. Ask everyone to unobtrusively choose one person to observe (but not stare at). On returning to base, have children describe their chosen person and someone can draw them or write brief observations. Help children fill out their character with an imaginary background. What job did they do? Where were they going? Why? Describe their home and family. Were they happy? What might happen to them? Fit the activity with a short, dramatic story about waiting, for instance the Bible story of Blind Bartimaeus waiting for a miracle (Mark 10:46–52). Use a made-up story about someone waiting for rescue, or show a clip from the BBC 999 programme. What do children think happened to these people afterwards?
- For any water-based activity, make sure you have experienced helpers and someone with life-saving qualifications. Use a public or private swimming-pool, with helpers and children acting, telling and

102

demonstrating the story of Naaman (2 Kings 5:1–27), the healing of the man at the pool (John 5:1–15), or the power of Jesus that enabled Peter to walk on the water (Matthew 14:29–36).

- Give groups of children the same story outline. Provide a range of rhythm and percussion instruments, and other utensils. Groups can explore telling the story with sound only, using instruments, voices, hands and feet. Groups can tell their story in turn to others.

- In advance, give everyone the same story, and assign characters to think about their part in the story. Have a TV presenter with a microphone interview the different characters, to ask what happened. Children give their point of view and tell their part of the story.

- With advance warning for preparation, have two helpers or older children debate a question. Afterwards, others must say who has persuaded them and why. Link this idea with 1 Peter 3:15 and discuss the reasons for the hope that Christians have.

- Choose a short story or Bible passage for its vivid description. Read it aloud twice. Children brush paper with water. The third time, read it slowly and, starting at the bottom of the paper, children can paint their chosen colours in strips for each part of the description or story. Everyone's painting should be different.

- Choose a chip shop with tables and seating. While children eat their chips, tell an improvised story around the table, with everyone taking a turn to add to the story. The story must include chip shop words.

Everyone who successfully inserts a word from the menu board into the flow of the story gains a chip from the other children.

- Check out your local library for a book on how to create cinquains, clerihews or Haiku poetry (see Notes on page 108). Show children simple examples, and explain how they work. Help children create their own to catch a moment from your story, or capture its essence, in the required number of syllables.
- Arrange a visit to a local sweet or chocolate factory. Make a list of all the names of the sweets or chocolates, keeping empty packets of freebies. Use the names of the sweets to brainstorm with children and helpers new ideas for made-up stories, link known films or stories, and Bible stories. Work at including everyone. Make several groups, each with a chosen story, to work on it and act it out, finding a useful application. Give an example.

When can I use stories?

Most children's work that takes place on a Sunday will already include Bible stories and teaching, and possibly other relevant life stories. The Children's Ministry Teaching Programme for 9–13+ gives a prominent place to Bible stories and teaching, using a four-year structured plan, and encourages children to focus on the application, and affirm it in their own lives. Some of the ideas in the previous section will probably not fit into a conventional

Sunday morning meeting with children, but others can be adapted and used effectively with whatever teaching material you use.

Storytelling enables children and adults to grow and mature in every way through truth, inspiration, imagination, vision and creativity. If storytelling has such enormous benefits, then opportunities need to be made for stories to be shared in a variety of age-appropriate forms, and at appropriate times. This is not just about juggling programmes, or trying to fit something extra into an already busy schedule for adults and children to struggle with. It may mean prayerfully re-thinking your current structures, making the best use of the time you have, or creating other times, be they occasional or frequent. Your situation is unique, and no one else can say what is right for you and the children in your care, but if you are convinced of the worth of storytelling, then you will find occasions and ways to tell stories. Ask God to help and show you how. Talk and pray with your leaders and helpers. Encourage and stimulate each other to produce an exciting arena for everyone to enjoy and grow through storytelling.

What stories can I tell?

Set yourself and your team a project. It may take a little time to complete, but will be an invaluable resource, and save much time later on. Also, it will be unique to you and the children in your group, and will be custom made for your children.

Ask children what kind of stories they enjoy. They will probably use TV and films as their source, as well as books. Make a list. It may include:

- adventure
- romance
- happy endings
- imperfect or perfect heroes or heroines
- fighting and battles
- conflict and resolution
- accusation and justice
- family sagas
- historical events
- fantasy
- explorers and pioneers
- sport
- sci-fi
- stories of people's lives
- crime
- murder
- pets and other animals
- environmental issues
- school life
- problems and difficulties to be overcome
- superheroes
- heroes of the faith
- stories with a twist in the tail.

Ask young people a little older than the children in your

group to add their ideas to your list. Add any vital topics you feel children have omitted.

Write each topic from your list on a separate page, and make three different headings: 'Bible stories', 'Made-up stories' and 'Fiction stories'. Working as a team with your leaders and helpers, or giving each team member a different part of the list, begin to research and investigate stories for each topic and heading. You are aiming to find at least one story idea for each topic under each of your three headings. More than one idea would be great, but you can add these over time. You may need to investigate your local children's library, school libraries and other people's bookshelves. Ask teachers and parents for ideas. A chain reference Bible would also be helpful.

The most difficult heading may be 'Made-up stories'. You can leave this until last. Look at the ideas given in chapter 4. If you or your team members don't feel confident about making-up your own stories, begin to search out those who are gifted to communicate in this way, but don't give up too soon on yourselves. You have more stories than you know inside you!

The following brief list or series may be worth looking at:

- *Bible Baddies*, Bob Hartman (Lion)
- *Fleabag and the Ring of Fire*, Beth Webb (Lion)
- *The Curious History of God*, Russell Stannard (Lion)
- *Don't You Wish*, Robin Jones Gunn. Sierra Jensen Series (Bethany House)

- *Narrow Walk*, Shirley Brinkerhoff. The Nikki Sheridan Series (Bethany House)
- *A Way Through the Sea*, Robert Elmer. The Young Underground Series (Bethany House)
- *Escape to Murray River*, Robert Elmer. Adventures Down Under Series (Bethany House)
- *The Thieves of Tyburn Square*, Dave and Neta Jackson. Trailblazer Books (Bethany House)
- *Heroes of the Faith Series* (Barbour)

Notes:

Cinquains are a form of poetry with five lines. The words chosen, and the form they take on the paper, are an important part of the writing. If given examples, some children will be able to express their thoughts verbally and visually through this medium.

Line one has one word to name the subject, e.g. Rollerblades.
Line two has two words to describe the subject, e.g. freedom, fun.
Line three has three action words about it, e.g. watching, risking, speeding.
Line four has a four or five word phrase that describes the subject. This is usually a thought, not a complete sentence, e.g. tingling danger rushing past.
Line five has one word that means the same as the first word, or a word that sums it all up e.g. joy.

Clerihews are a fun form of light verse named after their creator, Edmund Clerihew Bentley. They consist of two rhyming couplets of any length or metre. The first line usually contains the name of someone well known, fictional or genuine. The remaining lines capture the essence of the named person. Some children become very adept at creating clerihews, especially about their friends.

Example:

> Sir Christopher Wren
> Said, 'I am going to dine with some men.
> If anyone calls,
> Say I am designing St Paul's.'

Haiku is a Japanese form of poetry that follows a 5-7-5 syllable form.

Examples:

> Freckles all over,
> Ginger hair but very kind,
> Christopher my friend. (James Baker aged 10)

> Crashing at the cliffs,
> Then rolling away again,
> White horses prancing. (Megan Pocock aged 11)

However, seventeen syllables in English carry more information than seventeen syllables in Japanese. There is an English free-form Haiku that gives a short-long-short pattern without so rigid a structure. This makes it easier for children to create Haiku. Check out a Haiku website: www.tecnet.or.jp/~haiku/

7. Help! I've Got to Tell a Story!

It can be a very daunting prospect to be asked to tell a story. The first thing to remember is not to panic. You probably are more experienced than you think. Few people reach adulthood without having listened to stories read to them, having read stories for themselves, and even told stories to others in one form or another. Think how you enjoy being told a story, and keep those things in mind as you prepare yours. Recall any experiences of storytelling you have had in the past. These may have been direct storytelling to a group of people, or times that you may not have considered to be direct storytelling, e.g. telling jokes, sharing anecdotes, describing holidays or special events, recounting funny or sad things that happened.

Reading aloud versus telling a story from memory

You can be certain that by reading a story aloud:

- You will get it right.
- You will not leave out anything important.
- You don't need to try and remember every detail.
- You may be more confident with a book or written out story in front of you.
- Means it will still take practice, but less than telling a story without reading it.

Telling a story from memory:

- Makes it easier for you to make and keep eye contact.
- Helps you assess children's interest or lack of it, so that you can respond accordingly.
- Helps everyone become more involved in the story.
- Helps less confident readers.
- Means you will need more practice, especially with non-verbal skills and body language.

I've been told which Bible story to tell

- Can the story be read to children?
- Can you find a children's Bible story book to read it from?
- Can you write out the story simply in your own words and read it aloud?
- Will you tell the story in your own words from memory?

I have to choose my own Bible story

If you need it, ask for help to find a story with one clear, main theme. Complicated stories that take a long time to work out are hard to sustain. They may be very satisfying in the end, if everyone has worked out what has been going on, but children may drop out along the way.

Ideally, your story should contain drama, suspense and conflict. Look for a story that has an obvious beginning, middle and end. The beginning should set out the situation, predicament, conflict or emergency. The middle contains the building of tension, suspense and drama, working towards the climax, which should bring resolution.

Bible story example: Jesus calms the storm (Mark 4:35–41)

- **Beginning** – Jesus and the disciples set off across the lake in a boat. No sign of a storm. Jesus fell asleep.
- **Middle** – severe wind and rain set in. The waves were so high they threatened to swamp the boat and sink it. The disciples were afraid, even though some of them were fishermen, and used to storms. This was one of the worst. They were all going to be drowned. Somehow, Jesus stayed asleep. The disciples woke Jesus up, and accused Jesus of not caring about them.
- **Climax** – Jesus told the wind and waves to stop, and they did. Jesus told the disciples off for not trusting him to take care of them. The disciples were amazed at his power, and knew he was God's Son.

- **Point:** Jesus shows God's great power.
- **Application:** Jesus has power to take care of me.

Now it's your turn . . .

- Will you read your chosen story to children?
- Can you find a children's Bible story book to read it from?
- Will you write it out in your own words and read it?
- Can you write out the story in your own words and read it aloud?
- Will you tell the story in your own words from memory? You can hold the book or Bible in case you forget what comes next, or write out headline notes on cards, to help you remember it.

I have to tell a fiction story

If you are not familiar with children's fiction, then you will need to take advice. Visit your local children's library and ask for a shortlist of the most popular books for the age group you are dealing with. If you know any-one who teaches children in this age group, ask their advice too.

Read several examples through aloud, timing them and adding on a couple of minutes. Choose the one that you feel comfortable with, and think is the most suitable for your listeners and the length of time you have been given. Don't worry if children say they have heard the story already. Younger children especially enjoy repetition. Older children can be asked to listen carefully and tell afterwards why they think it is such a popular story for children of their age.

- Will you read your chosen story from the book?
- Will you write it out in your own words and read it?
- Will you tell the story in your own words from memory? You can hold the book in case you forget what comes next, or write out headline notes on cards to help you.

I have to make up my own story

Everyone has stories they can tell or put together from their own experiences, or from those of others. However, if you haven't done it before, it takes practice to get a story down on paper and knock it into shape. If you really need to tell your own made-up story:

- Keep it as short and simple as possible.
- Use the same principles as telling other good stories, by putting in some drama, suspense and conflict.
- Give it a good beginning, setting out the situation.
- Give it a middle, building the tensions, suspense and drama.
- Give it an end, to bring resolution.
- If you wish to bring out a point from your story, keep it brief.

- Make brief headline notes to help keep you on track as you tell your story.

What else might my story need?

Think about the ages and abilities of the children who will be listening. Look through previous chapters to see if there are one or two simple ideas you could include that would add another dimension to the story. To help you concentrate on the storytelling, ask someone to help you with the extras. Practise the story with them.

If you want to put your story into a setting, ask for help to think of ideas and to organise it. Some ideas are given in previous chapters. You have enough to do, telling the story.

Practise

Whatever kind of story you tell, and whichever method you choose to tell it, you will need to practise.

- Get to know your story inside out, even if you are going to read it aloud.
- Watch yourself read or tell it in a mirror. This will help get rid of any unhelpful mannerisms and facial expressions.
- Remember to smile and relax.
- Don't rush the story, and breathe evenly.
- Be enthusiastic about your story.
- Try to put in plenty of light and shade, fun and feeling.

What if it goes wrong?

We all make mistakes when storytelling, especially when we're very new to it. We may feel that the whole experience was a complete disaster. It rarely is as bad as that. Whatever happens, don't give up trying. We all improve in confidence and ability as we practise and keep improving. Often, children don't notice mistakes, and even if they do, they tend to be less critical than adults.

I forgot to say something really important!

If you forget to say something important, stop and say, 'Oh, I forgot something very important. . .' Tell what it was, and pick up the story again.

I started to waffle and lost children's attention!

As soon as you realise what has happened, stop and ask, 'Where was I before I got sidetracked?' Children can answer if they know. Go back to your last point, repeat it briefly and continue.

In practice, my story took ten minutes, but I finished it in five!

We speak quickly when we're nervous. Try to keep a steady pace and breathe evenly. Have an activity, song or rhyme ready that relates to your story, just in case you finish it too soon. For older children, prepare several brief questions, or let them tell the story back to you.

I completely lost children's attention!

If you lose children's attention and can't get it back, finish your story as quickly as possible and move on to the next item in your programme. Tell children you'll do better next time. Learn from the experience, but don't take it so seriously that you will never try again.

One of the children was frightened and started to cry!

Most children have vivid imaginations. Some are very sensitive and will easily identify with characters in your story. Think carefully about any frightening or emotionally sensitive parts, and try to find a balance between making them exciting and making too much of a drama about them.

If you see a child is upset, nominate a helper to comfort them. Talk to them afterwards and say you are sorry they were upset. Make sure they understand how the story worked out, and remind them of any good or funny parts of the story.

Afterwards, replay the storytelling experience in your head, however painful you think it was. Look for the good points and give yourself a pat on the back. Assess where you went wrong. Ask someone you trust from your team to tell you honestly but gently how you might improve. Don't give up. Storytelling may be scary, hard work, time consuming, disastrous or hilarious. It requires you to almost stand on your head, and do and be everything at once, to involve everyone in the story. But when you give it all you've got you will find it to be one of the most exhilarating and rewarding experiences of working with children.

Appendix

Discussion Topics

Use these questions on your own, with a colleague or during a children's workers' team meeting to stimulate discussion or consideration as to how to tell a story effectively in each situation.

1. If you had to tell the story of Peter's vision and visit to Cornelius' house recorded in Acts 10 to a group of 5–9s, how would you do it? Think about the story plan, your room or place setting, the storytelling style and any props you would use, and how to involve every child.

2. If you shared a room with another group, how would you tell a story to your 3–5s?

3. Think of a childhood experience, or imagine a time when you lost something very important to you. How could you make this into a brief, interesting story for a group of 6–8s? What point or application could you

bring out of your story?

4. If you had a child in your group of nine-year-olds who persistently tried to distract other children while you were telling a story, what would you do?

5. Make a list of books you enjoyed as a child in the three age groups covered by this book. Make another list of current books children in those three age groups enjoy today.

6. If you had to tell the story of the centurion's servant from Matthew 8:5–13 and Luke 7:1–10 to children aged 3–8, how would you do it?

7. If the person due to tell the story to your 7–9s telephoned to say they were ill and couldn't be there, what would you do?

8. How would you handle a group of three-year-olds who were distracted by a thunderstorm outside while you were telling your story?

Children's Ministry Teaching Programme

- Do you want to see children develop a personal relationship with Jesus?

- Do you want teaching sessions that are fun, biblical, evangelical and interactive?

- Would you like children to enjoy age-appropriate activities as they learn about God?

If you've said YES to any of these questions, you need the Children's Ministry Teaching Programme.

The Children's Ministry Teaching Programme provides four leader's guides covering ages from under 3 to 13+; KidZone activity books for children aged 5-7, 7-9 and 9-11; MiniKidz and KidZone craft books for children aged 3-5 and 5-9, a magazine for those over 11; a CD of music and stories; and FamilyZone with song words, ideas for all-age worship and parents' letters.

**For more information visit our web site
www.childrensministry.co.uk**

ENHANCING YOUR MINISTRY WITH CHILDREN